THEY WERE SENT

STAND APART FROM THE CROWD

How having an apostolic mindset can help you succeed as a leader in a hostile and volatile world.

For additional materials and books from
Dr. Matthew Kutz visit his website at
www.matthewkutz.com
or
Apostolic Team Ministries International
at **www.atmintl.org**

Apostolic Team Ministries International, Inc.

THEY WERE SENT
Stand Apart from the Crowd

Matthew R. Kutz

RTG Publishing
Division of Roundtable Group, LLC
Perrysburg, Ohio

Copyright © 2016 Matthew R. Kutz

No portion of this book – large or small - can be distributed, reproduced in any form, or stored in a retrieval system without the author's expressed written consent.

All scripture quotations, unless otherwise indicated, are taken from the *New King James Version*. Copyright © 1979, 1980, 1982 by Thomas Nelson, Inc. Publishers

Published by RTG Publishing
Perrysburg, Ohio

ISBN: 978-1-329-76922-9
1. Leadership. 2. Church Government. 3. Ministry.

Printed in the United States of America
Revised Edition   (11/6/16)

For my dad, a man sent from God. I miss you!

Acknowledgments

No book can ever come to fruition without the help and encouragement of others. That is certainly true in this case. My first draft of this book was penned nearly 13 years ago. Many drafts have come and gone and several people have taken the time to read the drafts and offer their input. Thank you to Pastor Gary King, Bill Fries, Dr. Ron King, and JC Alzamora for reading this manuscript in its previous stages. Your counsel and suggestions have not fallen on deaf ears.

I also thank my best friend and wife Angie! Who is been faithful to encourage me and support me not only in the preparation of this manuscript, but in many others and most importantly for supporting me and encouraging me. Angie, there are few other words that describe you as accurately as "awesome!" I love you!

Of course, few books take the time to acknowledge their readers. So to my readers I say thank you! Without you this would be a fruitless endeavor. I am truly appreciative that you have taken the time to read this book.

Table of Contents

Introduction		1
Part 1: Apostolic and Pastoral Models of Leadership		
Chapter 1	Old-School Leadership Development	6
Chapter 2	The Art and Science of Leading Well	20
Chapter 3	Pastoral and Apostolic Leadership	27
Chapter 4	The Apostolically-minded Leader	40
Chapter 5	The Leader as Shepherd	46
Chapter 6	What Shepherds do Best	56
Part 2: Apostolic Assignments of Old Testament Leaders		
Chapter 7	Apostolic Assignment of Adam	67
Chapter 8	Apostolic Assignment of Joseph	80
Chapter 9	Apostolic Assignment of Moses	100
Chapter 10	Apostolic Assignment of David	116
Chapter 11	Apostolic Assignment of Samuel	140
Chapter 12	Apostolic Assignment of Nehemiah	156
Chapter 13	Apostolic Assignment of Esther	170
Part 3: Enemies of Apostolic Assignments		
Chapter 14	Defending your Territory	181
Chapter Notes		195
Recommended Reading		197
About the Author		198

Introduction

I wrote the first draft of this book in 2002 as part of the requirements for my first Ph.D. I was excited about it then and 14 years later I am still excited about it. While much of the foundation of that original manuscript has remained the same, over the years my ideas and experiences have changed, which are now reflected in this book.

I had my first offers to publish this book in 2003, but something in my heart prevented me from following through. Even though I really wanted to have it published. I suppose deep down inside I believed it was a little presumptuous, for such an inexperienced man, to write a book on apostolic leadership.

Ironically, I have come to realize that I know even less today than I did then. I used to think that answering questions was a sign of good leadership. I've come to find out that anyone can answer questions and convey information. The true mark of leadership is being able to ask the right question, at the right time, to the right person!

If I have done my job correctly what is written on these pages will stir up more questions than they do answers. Good questions are harder to come by than most people realize. As you read this book don't just use it as a resource for information and ideas on leadership, but use it as a tool to aid you in your own discovery of what leadership is, how it is practiced, and most important of all, where it comes from.

So... take what is in these pages as the *unlearning* of leadership. Let me explain what I mean by unlearning. Somewhere along my formal education I came across the statement, credited to futurist and author Alvin Toffler, "The illiterate of the 21st century will not be those who can't read or write, but those who are unable to learn, unlearn, and relearn." It is the unlearning that so captivated my attention. We spend so much of our time as humans acquiring knowledge and gathering information. Thinking that the more information we have the better choices we will make and the more prepared we will be for whatever life brings us. The problem is nothing could be farther from the truth! Often times it is what we have worked so hard to learn that prevents us from seeing clearly what is right in front of us. Leadership – perhaps most of all – requires a continual cycle of learning, unlearning, and relearning. I hope that the words in this book will facilitate your *relearning* by helping you *unlearn* what you think you already know.

Who is this book for?

This book is not intended to be a scholarly attempt or a summary of research findings, or even best-practices on leadership. I have written textbooks and scholarly journal articles, but that is not what I want to do here. Not to imply that I have not done my best to diligently represent leadership or that those who are reading this are not serious students of leadership, much to the contrary. The rhetoric required for academic content bogs down and distracts from the simplicity in which leadership can and should be conveyed. However, I do intend this to be a serious and responsible investigation into the reality of leadership as it is modeled and demonstrated for us in the Old Testament. More specifically this book is intended to present a model of leadership that is unique to Christians. And, more specific than that one that is unique to Christians who pursue a life with the Holy Spirit. Implementing the principles outlined here can help you realize a greater level of success and favor in your leadership efforts regardless of the context in which you lead.

****

This book is divided into three parts. Part 1 is about leadership in general and is grounded in the words of the Apostle Paul from Romans 12:8, which states, "If God has given you leadership ability, take the responsibility seriously" (NLT). Leadership is a responsibility, which must be taken seriously and the Bible does have a lot to say about it. The rest of Part 1 is about leading well and distinguishing between pastoral leadership and apostolic leadership. I submit that it is an apostolic paradigm that is needed by today's Christian leaders. An apostolic paradigm is not about being an "apostle," but about believing you have been sent by God with an assignment that is unique to your gifts, anointing, and heritage.

Part 2 is about the apostolic profiles of Old Testament leaders. This is my favorite part of the book and its core. Part 2 is about the individual leaders and the different attitudes and actions that caused them to stand out above their peers and above even their masters. Many of these leaders not only functioned well in their environment but excelled in a world that was hostile to their beliefs and values. If you follow along with the lives of those outlined in Part 2 you will see how they had an apostolic paradigm, which enabled them to excel in foreign lands, in the face of adversity, under pagan masters, which is much like the business and marketplace many of us lead in today.

Part 3 is a chapter that summarizes how to defend your territory against enemies of your apostolic assignment. Make no mistake there are forces at work that would like nothing better than to see you fail. In Part 3 I look into what makes a good defense, what you are defending against, and specific tactics the enemy uses to render you ineffective. At the end of each chapter is a place for notes… please use them. Enjoy.

Part 1

If God has given you leadership ability, take the responsibility seriously. Romans 12:8 (NLT)

1

Old-School Leadership Development

One of my favorite movie lines of all time is from the animated Disney® movie *The Incredibles*. At the very end of the movie there is a scene where two old men witness the heroes overcome the odds and come together as a team to defeat the villain. One of the old men looks at the other one and says, "Now that's doing it old school." The second old man replies, "Yup, there's no school like the old school."

The old-school has nothing to do with being out-of-touch or antiquated. However, it is about doing something without shortcuts or offering excuses when something doesn't work out. The old school suggests that the best way to get something done is to take the time to do it right regardless of how inefficient it might appear. Being old-school has absolutely nothing to do with being antiquated, outdated, or irrelevant. In fact, doing it old-school can be cutting-edge; if based in a spirit of excellence.

Patriarchs of the Old Testament certainly qualify as coming from the *old school*. There were no seminaries, no *New York Times* best-selling books, no universities, no high-priced seminars or workshops for them to learn about leadership theories or explore management case studies. In fact, many of them never even intended to be leaders. God often sent them after He watched them work diligently. God had to visit them, convince them, and prove to them that as long as they obeyed they would be capable of leading extraordinary people in extraordinary ways. The leaders of the Old Testament – the ones that changed and shaped the world – and whose influence have lasted for centuries – learned leadership by trial and error; the old-school way, without shortcuts, after they demonstrated a strong work ethic. When something they attempted failed they often owned up to their failure, accepted the consequences, and tried again.

Do not misunderstand me, I believe there is plenty of room for formal education and mentorship – which are the other two ways you can learn leadership. But, if you really want a lesson to stick, nothing works better than introducing a little fear and allowing a little failure. This book is about some of the fear and failure that was part of their success. Leaders who were sent and ended up standing out in a crowd.

Ever since I was a young boy I have always admired leaders. I remember a regular tradition of sitting with my dad and watching the movie *Patton*, which starred George C. Scott. I used to think it was so boring and such a tedious event to sit there and watch it with him. However, as time went on I grew fonder of the movie and eventually began to recognize leadership. My father was also a student of the Civil War. There were always books around the house about famous generals, battles, and war strategies from that era. My dad would tell stories of heroic battles or a great leadership strategy that he recently read about. I have no doubt some of my fascination with leadership came from listening to his stories and watching him live his own life, which I am proud to say exemplified one of a humble leader and great man.

However, there is nothing that contributed more to my fascination with leadership than the stories I heard in Sunday school. Stories about Moses, Joseph, David, Nehemiah, Esther, and many others made leadership come to life to for me. Of course, these are not just kid's stories or myths, but real life accounts of men and women who led like they were called to lead, not always with the greatest of skill or intention, but with obedience and dependency. It was not their skill, but their obedience and dependence on God that enabled them to lead well.

Ever since those days with my dad and in Sunday school the ability to motivate, inspire, and accomplish objectives has always been something I have admired. I have always watched in amazement how some people routinely accomplish what they set out to do while others only seem to be able to hope that they get something done.

Leadership is something that God uses to strip away your dependency on anything but Him!

Ever wonder why that is? I think it has to with the skill set people choose to develop. Much of the world chooses to develop conventional leadership skills like empathy, initiative, communication, etc. What needs to be developed is our sense of interdependence, our track record of excellence, desperation for God, and obedience. These are skills that set leaders apart and when these are developed God can use you to lead. The conventional skills will eventually find their way into your larger skill set, but only after. It's ultimately about priorities. First, master the art of discipline, interdependency, excellence, and obedience; then the science of leadership can be explored.

From those days when I was a young boy till now, well over 30 years later, I have earned two doctorates on the subject of leadership, written a college textbook on the topic, written an award-winning book on the complexity of leadership, published dozens of papers and articles on the subject, and have presented and lectured on leadership related topics to a variety of organizations from small churches to Fortune 500 and global companies all over the world. Ironically, I am convinced I know less about leadership now than I ever have. Therefore, my disclaimer from earlier holds true. I'm not trying to teach you something new about leadership, but I'm hoping that what you read will cause you to ask more questions about it.

Developing Leaders

Developing leaders is one of the passions of my life and is something I believe God has equipped me to do. While I expect to have many more years of learning about leadership; which undoubtedly will help to refine my understanding of the concept, I can honestly say I have come to know leadership as a way of life and living. This way of living is far more valuable than knowing it as an academic pursuit. Many people lead out of what they read from books – what a tragedy. Leaders must learn to lead out of their sense of assignment and calling – and the models, best-practices, and theories found in books should only be a secondary tool.

Unfortunately, much of what is taught and disseminated in books about leadership is a theory. In these pages, I hope to be able to bring leadership to life for you as a process that God initiates to refine and shape us and hopefully you will come to know leadership as a way of life.

Leadership is not a title or position. Leadership is something that God uses to strip away your dependency on anything but Him! Leadership to man is an ambition it is something to acquire. On the other hand, I believe leadership from God's perspective is an instrument He uses to refine you and shape your personality and desires. After all, leadership is ultimately about being a faithful steward of the people that God has allowed you to serve.

I have had the privilege of serving in various leadership capacities in different local churches since 1996. I have served as a local elder (perhaps the most demanding of all the leadership roles I have held), I have worked on several church planting teams, some that failed and some that are succeeding, I have also served as an assistant pastor, church administrator, small group leader, and now a teaching pastor and director of an apostolic network. One thing is for certain and that is leadership is learned in day-to-day leading. Leadership is a journey that is never finished; it can never be bestowed upon someone in a single day.

Being promoted at work or ordained into ministry does not mean that the moment immediately preceding your promotion or ordination you were not a leader and then, as if by magic, the moment after the promotion or ordination you are now a leader. In actuality, you only just have been given formal responsibility to be a steward of something that belongs to God, which means you assume liability for the outcome. You will always only be a steward, but as you prove yourself obedient and faithful that stewardship can be a way to earn influence. There is a major fact that I want to make obvious about the idea of leaders as stewards, and that is ownership. Stewards recognize they are not the owner of what they are leading. With that knowledge, it frees them from many traps of conventional leadership roles.

Knowing about leaders and leadership is not the same as understanding what to do as a leader. The world is full of leadership-based "how to" books, but what the world needs are leaders who know "what to do." There is a distinct and dramatic difference in leaders who practice "how to" techniques learned from the pages of books to leaders who know "what to do" based on being led by the Spirit of God, experience, and wise counsel. Learning leadership by practice has been something that has been an incredible mystery to me that I have at times greatly enjoyed and at other times greatly despised.

Authentically Biblical Leadership

Leaders who model biblical values and have an intentional biblical worldview are needed in every industry and occupation around the globe. It is a tragic mistake to keep biblical leadership principles and techniques inside the four walls of the church. Leadership that is based on biblical ideals work; and they work well, and they work well everywhere.

That is not to say that you will not be ostracized or misunderstood for those values. To some biblical values are considered absurd, antiquated, superstitious, and ridiculous. For people who subscribe to that no amount of rhetoric or "proof" can change their minds. After all, it is as Paul said, "the carnal mind cannot perceive the things of the spirit." Quite simply their mind (intellect) is an obstacle that they cannot overcome. Moses confronted this with the Egyptian sorcerers. In spite of what appeared to be an obvious demonstration of the

Perfection is not possible in this life, but excellence is.

power and reality of God they refused to see it; and even thought they could mimic it.

We may not be able to convince everyone around us that biblical values are needed in our workplaces or are necessary for the practice of leadership, but what they do understand is performance. Having an authentically biblical leadership paradigm means that you are willing to be the best at what you do! The Bible is very clear that Jesus is the only one who lived a perfect life on the earth. Perfection is not attainable and God does not expect us to be perfect. On the other hand, God does expect excellence. Perfection is not possible in this life, but excellence is. Authentically biblical leadership is always excellent.

Apostolic Nuances

I use the term *apostolic* often. So, it is important to describe what I mean by it. Being an apostle and being apostolic are different. Just like being a leader, in the sense of being an owner or executive is different from an employee practicing leadership behaviors at work, at home, or in the community. Is everyone a leader? The answer is, yes and no. Yes, in the sense that everyone can practice and improve leadership behaviors. But no, in the sense that everyone can be an executive or owner. In this book I will be talking about being apostolic (or sent), not being an apostle. When we understand that we can be sent and embrace it we have a greater sense of purpose and access to authority. In summary, I believe anyone can aspire to be apostolic, but not to be an apostle.

The context of the principles and lessons outlined in this book are framed around what it means to be sent. To be sent by God is something special and unique. To understand that uniqueness requires a frame of mind that embraces a safer view of authority. A safer view of authority is simply the understanding that authority does not originate with you. Authority, in fact, is given only as long as it is used well. If abused, it can be taken away.

Apostolically-minded leadership is very unique; it is different from other forms or styles of leadership and should be differentiated from pastoral leadership, business leadership and management. We will discuss what differentiates them in more detail later, but it is necessary to be acutely aware that all sent leaders are also shepherds, but not all shepherds are sent.

To be sent means to operate out of a different level of authority, which is always delegated. It is the concept of *delegation* that I most wish to emphasize here! Being truly sent is always – that's right, I said "always" – delegated. That means the authority came from somebody and somebody can take it away! I do not believe God will take away your gift, but authority and assignments can be removed. I believe this is the reason why those who are sent stand alone as a different kind of leader with a different kind of motivation. Their motivation is to build something for someone else and once built steward it. As opposed to building something for themselves with ownership in mind.

The most accurate contemporary description we have for what it means to be sent is a naval admiral. An admiral is a commander of a fleet of ships– not just one ship, but many ships. The purpose of deploying those ships is to colonize new territories. Those territories where not to come under the rule or government of the admiral, but of the king or sovereign who commissioned the fleet. Likewise, as stewards, we should not seek independent or autonomous authority but delegated authority.

I believe we get a better picture of "sentness" and delegated authority when looking into the lives of Old Testament leader's. The New Testament description of apostolic ministry is foundational, but without the Old Testament to help us we might get an incomplete picture. The bible in its entirety is where our picture of this type of leadership should come. When we look into the Old Testament to supplement what we already know of New Testament apostolic ministry we get a unique perspective on what it takes to be sent. Pastors likewise will practice leadership from their experience and their ministry, it is not wrong or incorrect, only different; evangelists do the same, so do administrators, so do educators, so do business owners. Every believer was commanded to go (Matthew 28:16-20). In other words, every believer is, sent. Therefore, understanding the principles and practices of others who have been sent can be applied to us, regardless of our gift, passion, or ministry.

Specifically, my goal is to present a framework of leadership based on the practices, circumstances, and frame-of-mind (if you will allow me to presume I can guess the frame-of-mind) of leaders in the Old Testament who were sent. That statement is the first (of what I am sure will be many) debatable statements, but if you can handle this one I encourage you to keep reading as I explain this statement.

The word apostle does not appear in the Old Testament. Furthermore, as far as I know no Old Testament character was ever referred to as an apostle. Apostle is a uniquely New Testament term. How then can I say that I am framing my main idea on the concept of "Old Testament apostles?" Well... that is exactly what I intend to explore and is a question I believe can be explained without violating the integrity of biblical interpretation or biblical principles.

What does it mean to be apostolic?

Are all leaders' apostles? No! But, what if they are CEO's, gifted and called to teach and equip, and have uncanny favor and influence at work, still the answer is, No! Are all apostles' leaders? Yes. I believe true, authentic apostles are sent to exercise authority in the church.

Marketplace Christians can be apostolic, but unless they are recognized by a local church eldership they are not apostles. On the other hand, to be apostolic only means you are sent, and may or may not, function as an apostle to the church. Being apostolic means you feel a sense of obligation to steward another's interests. Apostolic leaders understand that authority is not their own, and whoever or whatever they are assigned to steward is not their own. Being sent merely implies authority to operate in your sphere. And, the fact that you are *sent* should be cause to adjust your thinking about your mission, gifting, talents, and behaviors.

This is primarily a book about how all Christians should practice leadership as ones who have been sent. This reality should be incredibly liberating and instill a sense of purpose and passion in your work. If true, this means you are in a God-ordained ministry and don't need a formal church leadership job to fulfill your calling. As I have said, I do not contend that everyone with a leadership calling is (or can be) an apostle. Therefore, I believe that the concept of "sentness" is not confined to the pages of the New Testament. When Christians begin to do their work and live life as if sent by God to do it, it adds new meaning and purpose. This new meaning and purpose cause you to stand out in the crowd. It draws attention to you, which as a steward, is easy to redirect back toward God.

There is little biblical evidence that New Testament apostles were sent to any place other than the church. Therefore, I subscribe to the belief that the Church is the context where apostles are recognized; that is until I see Fortune 500 companies paying CAO's (Chief Apostolic Officers) instead of CEO's or presidents to lead them. I do believe that you can be apostolically-minded and *sent* and not be an apostle.

In a similar way, I believe every believer should know and recognize God's voice, but not every believer is a prophet. Every believer should be able to "rightly divide the word of truth," but not every believer is a teacher. Likewise, every believer is "their brother's keeper," but not everyone is a pastor. Finally, every believer is to be a "living epistle known and read by all men," but not all are evangelists.

Being apostolic means you feel a sense of obligation to steward another's interests.

It is from this perspective that I believe all believers are sent, but not all are apostles. If I didn't believe that, it would be impossible for me to argue that Old Testament leaders functioned in an apostolic assignment.

Apostles in the Church only?

I believe New Testament apostles were intended to function in the church (1 Corinthians 12:28). Furthermore, Ephesians 2:19 – 20 implies that it is the church – and not businesses or entrepreneurial endeavors – that is built on the foundation of apostles (and prophets). While there are believers who have marketplace assignments and are sent to minister outside of the church I believe it is a mistake to refer to them as marketplace-apostles. They may be sent-Christians and even have an apostolic assignment, but to call them apostles is misleading. You may be tempted to say, "come on Dr. Kutz, isn't that just semantics?" No, it is not. To be an apostle is to be recognized by the leaders in the local church and peers, which is normally preceded by a public laying on of hands and commissioning from a local body of church elders to build the church and edify the saints. Authority to function and even rule in the marketplace is not equivalent to building the church or edifying the saints. In fact, many people in the marketplace are not even saints, in any sense of the word.

However, there are aspects of the apostolic mandate and an apostolic "frame-of-mind" that are relevant and useful for every Christian, that fact is borne out in the lives of the Old Testament leaders. In other words, while the technical role of the apostle is only found in the New Testament the concept of apostolicity (or sentess) is found throughout the Bible. It is from this basic understanding that I have identified certain Old Testament leaders as having been sent. In other words, each of the Old Testament leaders we discuss were in some way sent by God to lead. They practiced leadership through the lens of their apostolic assignment or sentness, but often operated in other gifts. This is what I believe it means to be an apostolically-minded leader; to demonstrate the requirements of leadership being fully convinced that God has delegated to you the authority necessary to make a difference. Most often that difference is made in the lives of people who work in the place they were sent. Often that difference is felt in the organization itself. Sometimes the difference is also felt in the community they are sent to or even the industry.

There are plenty of good books on apostles and the apostolic ministry and I have recommended some in the back of this book. I hope this book spurs you on to study the life, times, and ministry of the New Testament apostles. It is a worthy endeavor. There is much to learn about fathering, church planting, and church government by studying the New Testament apostles – but you can do that at a different time with different books.

Some of the Old Testament leaders we will explore were sent by God and some were sent by men, but they all were sent to do a work for God by someone with a greater level of authority than their own. I believe that the very fact that they were sent (what I have already referred to as their "sentness" or "apostolicity") gives them unique authority to accomplish the assignment for which they were sent. Likewise, when we receive an assignment from God (are sent), which is often determined by our passion, to go into a particular realm or sphere in the world we too are equipped with and delegated a certain level of grace and authority to accomplish that assignment. Sometimes it is a perpetual authority and other times it is only temporary for a specific task. Regardless, our sentness gives us an unfair advantage (cf. Psalm 119:99).

I believe that by examining the lives of those who were sent we can gain valuable insights and useful tools to implement into our lives that will help us accomplish the call of God and fulfill the purpose for which we were sent. Each one of the leaders we will examine had aspects of their lives, which when recognized and practiced by us today can lead to greater effectiveness in whatever capacity we lead, and will enable us to stand out in a crowd.

But, before we examine these Old Testament leaders I think it is necessary to make a distinction between the leadership practices within an apostolic paradigm and other paradigms. I believe that an apostolic paradigm requires a different way of thinking relative to leadership development. I am advocating for old-school leadership development by differentiating some of the nuance of the apostolic authority demonstrated by Old Testament leaders to the more contemporary leaders we see emerging on the scene today.

2

The Art and Science of Leading Well

Much has been written about leadership. In fact, so much has been written about leadership it is easy to lose the essence and character of leadership. I believe the essence of leadership can be summed up into two descriptive words; influence and productivity. In other words, those who demonstrate leadership get things done by ethically motivating and inspiring others to help them. They use a diversity of gifts, attitudes, talents, skills, and behaviors to do it, but in the end – they get "it" completed. Whatever "it" is they find the right way to see it completed. Note that I did not say they find *any* way to get it done. The best leaders get it done the right way – and the right way is always God's way. They realize that the end does not justify the means.

How a leader goes about accomplishing something is just as important as accomplishing it. Consider Moses who in getting water from the rock was commanded to speak to the rock, yet in his frustration, he struck the rock. The water came out – he got *it* done – but God was still displeased with how he accomplished his task. In the end that presumption cost Moses dearly!

When leadership becomes about getting it done *the right way* it changes the leadership-candidate pool. It is a common assumption that leadership can be demonstrated by anyone anywhere (and I do not disagree), but when you include the caveat of "the right way" there is a higher standard implied. And unfortunately not everyone aspires to that standard.

From an apostolic paradigm it's not enough to just get it done. In fact, many times high profile positions or desirable titles are given to someone because they already are exhibiting leadership excellence. I believe one must diligently practice leadership before you can become the leader. The irony of that is even if you never are recognized as a formal leader you may still be blessed because of the leadership you are demonstrating. Practicing leadership the right way has intrinsic rewards, even if you are never publicly recognized for it.

Because of this distinction between leader and leadership, it is necessary to view leadership as an art and a science.

The Art

As art, leadership is subject to different interpretations. In other words, leadership is subject to the artist's whims, attitudes, and preconceived notions of the world, which does not guarantee that the observer will interpret or view the art as the artist intended. This is what can make leadership so confounding and difficult to grasp. Therefore, the student of leadership must be willing to re-interpret and re-evaluate their craft often. In other words, leadership requires frequent and sometimes dramatic adjustments. Ironically, it is often this ambiguity that makes leadership such an enjoyable experience for some and so painful for others.

For example, it is very plausible that one can read certain passages of Scripture – say Exodus 18 – and conclude that like Moses, leaders create teams, oversee teams, and delegate differing levels of responsibility to team members. And therefore – rightfully – believe that the team is something that is set up to assist and serve the leader. This is in fact very biblical! On the other hand one can read certain passages of Scripture – say Acts 13 or 15 – and conclude – rightfully – that team leadership grows internally out of an established team of peers. Both perspectives are in fact biblical. The truth of both passages – when considered together – is that leadership is shared by a plurality of elders! Whether it is shared from the top down – vertically – or among peers – horizontally – is an issue of artistic interpretation. Granted I will concede that it has very practical implications on day-to-day work, but perhaps this is the first area requiring some unlearning and relearning, that I referenced earlier.

The Science

On the other hand, as a science leadership is a serious business. Like any science, the science of leadership is dependent upon certain stable conditions in which to observe and measure predictable outcomes. Therefore, leadership must have a solid foundation of assumptions that the leadership practitioner can use to stand upon. Without stable or predictable assumptions of reality, there is no basis on which to build, after which it becomes impossible to teach or pass on meaningful lessons. It is now clear that leadership operates on a continuum, a very long continuum; on one side is the art, the unpredictable, the ambiguous, on the other side is the science, the stable, the measurable, and the constant. The science of leadership is seen in Paul's teaching to Timothy. The characteristics Paul outlined in 1 Timothy 3 are non-negotiable. As such they are scientific, in the sense that they are stable, observable, and measurable.

It is as if leadership – like life – is a dance between embracing Newtonian-based physics, which requires a stable, predictable, and sequential order and quantum physics, which requires embracing complexity, chaos, and non-linear patterns. The first lesson of leadership is to balance the art and science of that continuum.

Leadership Principles

Much biblical exegesis and scientific research has gone into the study of leadership and I am grateful for that, but good leadership is not formed or developed from a book, nor can it be proven effective in a lab. The world is too unpredictable and not even close to "lab-like" conditions. There is no patent on good leadership; there are good models available to study and learn from, but no one model can claim to be the best, no one leadership principle or law can claim to be superior.

Managers can be developed in the classroom, but leaders are developed in the crucible of life.

A principle should transcend time, cultures, and geography. As an art, leadership is different from place to place and people to people. The only constant to effective and productive leadership is fluidity. Each leader must be able to adapt and flow in whatever environment they find themselves in. Therefore, principles of leadership should transcend the context in which they are practiced. In this respect leadership does not consist of the idiosyncratic nuances or technical competencies of a given industry or job – albeit these are important for a myriad of other reasons and should never be neglected. In light of this, much of what is considered leadership "principles" should be reduced to the status of a "model." Books and strategies must, therefore, be scrutinized, not as laws or principles, but only as ideas, suggestions, or models that may not work in every environment or in every situation. The wise student takes what is applicable and uses it, what is not applicable can be modified or thrown out.

No one person can merely pick up a book, study the topic of leadership and then rise to greatness as a leader. Books and research are beneficial, but it is the Word of God that is the "lamp unto our feet and the light unto our path." Today's leaders must use the inspired and revelatory Word of God as the primary source of direction – it is the only key that works every time!

Leadership is much more than knowledge, good communication, strategic planning, and managing conflict. Those skills are very necessary, they can make one a much better manager or administrator, but alone is not leadership. Furthermore, leadership for those who are sent is more than influence. Influence is essential, but it is only the beginning; sent leaders must also know what direction they are facing and where they are headed. Influence is worthless if you do not know what direction you are going or how to use it ethically. Leadership status is not "confirmed" solely on your level of influence. Effective leadership is based on going where God directs. Even if you influence thousands you can lead them nowhere or worse take them to the wrong place.

The Church is not always recognized, nor given its rightful respect as the training ground that it is.

Ultimately, influence must give way to authority. In the business of leadership, and especially being sent, leaders are called and gifted by God, given authority and, therefore, must rely on the Holy Spirit to guide them. This is different from managing.

Managers are given their positions to maintain the status quo, which implies no movement at all, but to ensure stability. People can be trained, equipped and educated to be great managers, but there is a vast difference between this and leaders. Leaders are developed too, and sometimes in the same way, but always managers help by ensuring people stay put and leaders help by ensuring people move forward. Managers can be easily developed in the classroom, but leaders are developed in the crucible of life.

Leadership and the Church

It is now more necessary than ever that the Church begin to develop leadership strategies based on apostolic thinking; to do that the Church must be led by men and women who have been sent; leaders with authority, not managers or program administrators. Yes, the world desperately needs administrators and managers, but not at the expense of leaders who are charged and sent by God, and equipped with authority to lead.

I am a product of the local church, my theological and ministry training is far better and has much more depth because of my service and ministry in the local church – yes, I have a formal education (too much actually and sometimes gets in the way of common sense), but most of the time the value I offer as a leader is based on my experience in the local church, not my education. I love the local church and the entire body of Christ. I believe that the Church is the gate of God (Gen 28:17) and that it is the mystery and difficult path that leads to life (Matthew 7:14). As such, the Church is not always recognized, nor given its rightful respect as the training ground that it is. One can learn innumerable and significant lessons that can only be attained from serving the local church. I am not against education, in fact, I am very much for it, but one cannot underestimate the power and impact of serving in the local church on the making of the leader.

Today the world needs leaders who come from, arise from, and are forged in the context and framework of the local church. Seminaries and colleges cannot produce the caliber of leader that is needed in every industry across the globe, but if we can submit ourselves to it and to the leaders in it, the church can provide the leaders the world needs, leaders who will stand out in the crowd.

3

Pastoral and Apostolic Leadership

Before we delve into the nuances of pastoral leaders and apostolic leaders I want to clearly state that I believe everyone who is sent must learn to shepherd! They do not need to have a spiritual gift or calling as a pastor, but they must learn to love, appreciate, and serve God's sheep. Sent leaders must never forget that they will always be their brother's keepers. It would be ludicrous to believe the sent leader is exempt from studying the Word because they are not gifted as a teacher. Likewise, it is ridiculous for any sent leader to think that they don't have to care for the flock or be considerate of people just because shepherding is not there primary gifting. In fact, I believe that a prerequisite for an apostolic assignment is to first love, defend, and feed God's sheep. When an apostolic assignment distracts from caring for people something has gone seriously awry; and if that is the case any wise person should question the legitimacy of that assignment!

While all sent leaders must learn to shepherd the reverse is not necessarily true! Not all shepherds need to be or should be apostolically-minded. With that said – and I hope that raises a few questions for your own contemplation – let's delve into the role of the pastor-shepherd in the local church.

Pastor-Shepherds

Few leaders are as unrecognized and underappreciated as pastors, and fewer roles require more leadership savvy than pastoring. Being a pastor is hard work. I have been fortunate in my life to have had – and still have – great pastors to guide and protect me. Over the years, a majority of what I've learned about leadership has not come from books or college courses, but from observing these pastors on the front lines.

The intent of this chapter is to delineate the differences between pastoral leaders and sent leaders. Not that pastoral leaders can't be sent, they can be, but typically their motivation and behaviors are different. I want to be crystal clear that I in no way intend to imply pastoral leadership is inferior. In fact, without pastoral leadership, the apostolic model of leading would be significantly one-sided and dysfunctional. With that being said, I believe the church and the marketplace need more apostolically-minded leaders. Much in the same way that families need to have fathers more involved.

When an apostolic assignment distracts from caring for people something has gone seriously awry.

I absolutely love Romans 12:8; it has become one of the hallmark mottos of my life. The Apostle Paul says that the gifts that are given to mankind differ according to each person. In light of leadership (and the other gifts) two things stand out here, 1) gifts are given, and 2) they differ in amounts. Meaning two people may get the same gift, but may have differing levels of that gift. Paul goes on to list several gifts and then mentions that there are those who are gifted to rule and that they should do so with diligence[1]. In this case, diligence can mean, with serious intent. In other words, if you have the gift of leadership you better use it and you had better be serious about developing it.

A close examination of the 12th chapter of I Corinthians reveals the same principle. The word rule in the Greek is *proisteômi* and is taken from the two words "*pro*" and "*histemi*" and means to stand before[2]. It carries the idea of first in rank or to preside, be over, or rule. Other translations translate this word as lead or leadership. The idea that leadership is only for those called or gifted to lead is becoming less popular as research about it unfolds and competency-based models gain popularity. Most people (and even leaders) agree that everyone can practice leadership somewhere. However, it is silly not to acknowledge that some will "naturally" be more efficient and effective at leading than others. However, even though everyone has the opportunity to demonstrate leadership that does not necessarily mean that someone cannot be born or gifted with leadership ability. I believe there are those (according to Romans 12:8) who are born with the gift to lead or rule. While everyone can certainly assume a lead role in specific situations and make improvements to their leadership skills, we must be careful not to ignore the distinction the Bible places on the gift of leadership.

This understanding can help us identify differences between "born leaders" and "made leaders." A pastorally-minded paradigm allows for church leaders to be made on a man-made timeline. An apostolically-minded perspective does not allow for this. It holds to the belief that leadership, while needing to be developed is placed there by God, and no amount of man-made theories or concepts can accelerate God's process. If indeed what John Maxwell says is true, and I believe it is, that, "everything rises and falls on leadership[3]," then it becomes essential that the correct, God ordained, and gifted person assume the leadership role God intended for them to assume.

This is significant regardless of the context. The church is not the only place where leadership needs to be demonstrated effectively. Exercising leadership in roles outside of the church also requires giftedness and diligence. And, apostolically-minded people are best suited to do this even outside of the church.

It is at this point that I believe the second distinction between pastoral leadership and apostolic leadership can be made. While it is true that the ministry of the apostle – I believe – is restricted to the local church, I do also believe – and it is not a contradiction – that the apostolic mindset of being *sent* transcends the church and should be practiced in the marketplace. The marketplace needs Christians who believe they have been sent there by God to affect change. Without a sense of assignment, it is easy to quit or find other means to express your passion and gifting. This is very much like a pastor who does not feel called to a particular church or people – the Bible refers to them as a hireling – and at the first sign of trouble they leave or transfer elsewhere. Pastors must feel a sense of duty and obligation – based on

> *Pastoral leaders bring people to the church, but sent leaders take the church to the people.*

a calling – to the people over whom God has called them to steward. When that sense of duty and obligation is present leaving in the face of trouble is very difficult. Marketplace leaders, likewise, must feel a sense of sentness.

Pastorally minded leaders are most effective within the local church or parachurch organizations and minister to a specific body of believers. It is the believer that needs the unique ministry of the pastor. In other words, pastoral leadership is practiced by Christians to Christians in the context of ministry. This is not to say that the world does not need pastoral care. It most definitely does. I believe it is the responsibility of every Christian in the marketplace to nurture and care for their fellow man. But the behaviors, motives, and attitudes of pastorally-minded leaders is unique to what Christians need. To be even more specific pastorally-minded leaders are uniquely qualified and gifted to care for, encourage, nurture, and lead those believers who have been sent into the marketplace to do what God has called them to do outside of the church.

When leaders demonstrate pastorally-minded leadership to everyone outside the context of the church confusion often is the outcome. The people in the competitive and demanding context of the global marketplace in an ungodly world don't need pastorally-minded leaders to lick their wounds for them, pat them on the back, and tell them that everything is going be all right. They need that, but they need that from the church. Christians who are in the marketplace are best suited for that role and when Christians come alongside their colleagues and offer their support it draws their colleagues toward the church. What the global marketplace needs are apostolically-sent leaders, who will not necessarily lick wounds and pat backs, but blaze trails, colonize territories, and direct people to the church where they can receive the help they need from pastorally-minded leaders. In other words, pastoral leaders bring people to the church but sent leaders take the church to the people.

First Timothy 3:2-7 lists several attributes required of shepherds that have little to do with giftedness. Interestingly, the "gift to lead" is not listed among them. It is tempting to add that requirement, but adding to the list something not there is the basis of legalism. Most of the attributes Paul lists for Timothy are issues of character and integrity. Therefore, it is possible that pastors do not need the gift of leadership to be effective in their ministry, but apostles do.

I believe Paul's list is of leadership behaviors in general and since he is talking to leaders it is implied he means leadership. Having good character qualifies you to shepherd others, and Paul even writes that it is good to desire the office of bishop (overseer), but having the desire and character necessary to shepherd does not automatically suppose you are a good and qualified leader in the sense of Romans 12. Later in Paul's pastoral epistle to Timothy, he writes that there are those who "rule well," implying a difference, a higher level of leadership ability distinct from those "who rule." It important to note that all shepherds may not be leaders, but all leaders should shepherd. Pastoral leadership and apostolic leadership are not necessarily mutually exclusive in practice, but they are different.

Part of the responsibility and passion of a true God-called leader is their heart toward the people God has placed them with. They must have a strong desire to see the sheep whole, healthy, and prosperous in the things of God. Moving people into this type of relationship involves some serious shepherding on the part of the leader.

It is widely accepted that leadership skills can be acquired. While this is certainly true, it must not be forgotten that leadership is more than a job to aspire to. Leadership is more than the summation of skills, training, and experience. The obsession with academia as the standard of training has seriously hurt our local churches. Academia is a useful tool, but it is only one tool in a box of hundreds of tools and it should never trump servanthood.

Consider Moses, he was a man called to lead from his mother's womb; but if God had not fashioned him in Pharaoh's court – his initial learning process – or as a shepherd in Midian – his unlearning process – he would not have been qualified to lead Israel through the desert – his relearning process – despite his calling.

Moses required all three experiences: 1) learning, 2) unlearning, and 3) relearning in order to fulfill his leadership calling. If his only training occurred in Pharaoh's court, he would have been completely unable to lead Israel through what they had to go through. Becoming a leader is similar to the "called and chosen phenomenon." Many leaders are called, but few endure the unlearning and relearning process required to be qualified and chosen as leaders.

Does the church need business principles?

What motivates a church should be entirely different than what motivates a business or a corporation. This is the basis for the third distinction between pastorally-minded leaders and sent leaders. While the church has some business aspects to it, it is not a business. The church must require that its pastors operate its leadership principles from an entirely different frame-of-mind than contemporary organizational behavior or modern management models. This frame of mind should include principles based on the observation and assessment of biblical examples and teachings.

When a church sends away their most capable young people to learn leadership from academic institutions whether secular universities or seminaries it hurts. Originally thought to be helpful it is proving to be more detrimental. By referring people out to be trained the church has abdicated its responsibility to train and equip leaders! Businesses and organizations do not need more leaders with Ivy League MBA's they need leaders who were trained and equipped in the local church. Businesses need leaders who learned leadership by serving alongside others in a local church who are able to bring a different picture of what an organization can be – not just a revenue-generating source of income for shareholders – but a family of covenantal people. Likewise, churches and ministries do not need experienced business leaders to come and save them, they need leaders called, ordained, and sent by God. I believe most Christian leaders are meant for the marketplace, but must be called, equipped, and sent by the church.

The church must export biblical leadership principles to the marketplace and not import them from the market-

Leadership theorists, sociologists, and psychologists have produced many materials on leadership and management for the corporate setting, admittedly some (but certainly not all) are suitable for local churches and offer valuable insight. However, the Church is unique and the leadership principles, which govern it, should also be unique, which creates a formidable tension in how its leaders are trained. That tension is rooted on the question, if the church uses one kind of leadership philosophy and world needs a different kind – can the church equip people to do both? Is the church a place where leadership can be developed for everyone, specifically those who are not called to be or desire to be leaders "in the church?" In other words, can the Church, with is different leadership mindset effectively train leaders to lead outside of the church, say in the business or media industries? Of course it can!

One reason it can is because the Church's paradigm transcends context. Biblical principles can be effective and useful in the marketplace, but secular principles (ideas and actions not based on faith or principles not breathed on by the Holy Spirit) cannot be used in the church.

Webster's dictionary defines a paradigm as "a philosophical and theoretical framework of a scientific school or discipline within which theories, laws, and generalizations and the experiments performed in support of them are formulated." Simply put a paradigm is a worldview; it is the lens through which we see things. Therefore, it becomes increasingly important that our worldview is correct. The lens, through which we see things, most of all leadership, must be that of Holy, God-breathed, inspired scripture and the Holy Spirit.

We must not use a secular worldview to operate or lead in the church, but you can and should use a biblical worldview to operate and lead in the world. Therefore, teaching leadership in the church is necessary for both the church and the marketplace.

The Church must recognize that many of the leadership models it imports are based on paradigms foreign to the mission of the church. The church must *export* biblical leadership principles to the marketplace and not *import* them from the marketplace.

In the secular marketplace, much of what is taught about leadership is centered on making money or producing a product. The Church is not in this business. The Church is about establishing the Kingdom of God and promoting Jesus Christ. I know… I can hear many of you saying to yourselves, "but Dr. Kutz the church needs money to do ministry and operate its programs so that the community can be blessed..." True. But, the church is not primarily a financial institution nor is it in the business of making a profit or producing revenue. Money is a tool for ministry not a driving motivation behind ministry.

The Church is primarily a life-giving organism, not a delivery-centered organization. Therefore, the theories of leadership that are woven into the Church must be evaluated differently. What is the difference? The Church is first and foremost a family, not a corporation. The family mentality and all that goes with it, relationship, covenant, loyalty, compassion, mercy, grace, and "tough love" to name a few are the basis and underlying theme of church leadership. The leaders that the world and church need must be sent out and commissioned by a higher authority. Business schools, universities, seminaries, and seminars or workshops simply are not capable of equipping someone for an apostolic assignment.

In a family as opposed to a business, a different set of rules apply. When someone in your family displeases you or fails, you do not "write them up," fire them, or send them to human resources for sensitivity training. When a family member does not follow through and deliver what was promised, you cannot switch relatives like you switch vendors. Capitalism and competition should not be the driving force behind the Church. In a family, a problem, whatever it is, must be worked out; separation is not an option. There is a greater sense of commitment, a bond that helps us when separation seems like the only option. This bond and commitment is called covenant. The Church deals in covenant while the world's leadership systems deal in contract. Contracts have loopholes and can be abolished or broken. Contracts are simply not binding, covenant is everlasting!

Covenant leadership says that, "I am committed to you and to this place. I will not leave and you cannot kick me out." Much like the institution of a Christ-based marriage, what God has joined together, let no man put asunder.[6] Serving in the church is the only place where this can be learned. In a nutshell, to be apostolically-minded means that you embrace being trained and equipped in a local church.

Covenant-based leadership (the heart of both the pastoral and apostolic leadership) goes two ways. Leadership does not give up on you, and you do not give up on leadership. This can be freeing for both, with a commitment to help, encourage, promote and support each other everyone is free to fulfill their God-given roles and abilities. Having God-ordained leaders in the Church could help ensure that the body is truly being fitted together and having each joint supply what is needed (Ephesians 4:16). For this type of leadership to take place, there must be recognition by both parties that God is involved in this process, and that He has sent certain people – often it is a plural team – to the local church to help lead.

****

In the next two chapters, I will describe the apostolic leadership paradigm and the pastoral leadership paradigm, respectively. It is important that I remind you that I am not comparing and contrasting the apostolic leadership paradigm and the pastoral leadership paradigm to imply that one is better than the other.

I am merely pointing out that the motivation and drive behind the two are different – and that one is more appropriate than the other relative to context. It should be noted that many times the results or outcomes of these two paradigms end up being the same. For example, apostolic leaders and pastoral leaders both want people to feel empowered and to succeed in whatever they put their hand to do. But they each may go about accomplishing this in a different way. Only the context determines which one is appropriate. And, indeed, it is true that one person can demonstrate both.

The main difference is often about motivation and perspective behind their behavior and not the technique used to achieve the goal. Sent leaders and pastoral leaders may even use the same or similar techniques and have similar experiences. An analogy between a father and a mother may be helpful here. As parents, both the father and the mother, have goals, dreams, and aspirations for their children. However, it doesn't take too much insight to recognize that how a father goes about accomplishing these things and how a mother may go about accomplishing these things can be quite different. Both parents hope for the same outcome, but one uses hugs and kisses and the other uses the "pull-yourself-up-by-the-bootstraps" technique.

Both the apostolic and shepherding leadership paradigms can be very effective and if you are a pastor then by all means chapter 5 and the shepherding leadership paradigm is essential for you to embrace and understand. But if the church is truly going to train and equip leaders to promote and advance the kingdom of God in the marketplace it needs to equip and train leaders from an apostolic paradigm.

***

One more note – I want you to understand that I will not draw the distinctions for you, I will present each chapter (4 and 5) as if it is the way leadership is supposed to be. I will leave it to you to see and recognize any differences.

4

The Apostolically-Minded Leader

The church is seeing a return of the apostolic ministry. Despite how you may feel about the title "apostle" or those individuals who call themselves apostles the work of an apostle is needed. Over the years, there have been many different labels placed upon this ministry: church planter, missionary, evangelist, or senior pastor, regardless of the term, the name is not as important as the function. The Bible calls them apostles; so I will too. I understand that the title apostle can be disconcerting to some. I agree that its capacity to be abused and misused is greater than other "titles," so let's not bother with the name itself (let's save that for another time and place) what is important is the function.

As stated earlier, it is not my purpose to write on apostles or the apostolic ministry, but some general statements are necessary to help us understand what it is I am saying about those who are *sent* in these next pages. For sure apostolically-minded leaders must love, protect, and promote the sheep. In that sense, I believe that all legitimate apostolic ministry understands the necessity to shepherd. However, apostolically-minded leaders are motivated differently and employ different techniques and strategies than pastors.

Apostle is a New Testament word, used by Paul, and means to be sent or sent one, and has the connotation of an ambassador or admiral of the naval fleet. While it is a New Testament word, it is not exclusively a New Testament concept. The Old Testament had several "apostolic" types. The Hebrew word that is translated apostle in the Septuagint is *shalach* and it means sent or sending. In the Old Testament we find that several people were sent: Moses, Joseph, Abraham, Jeremiah, Samuel, Nehemiah, Esther, and Elijah to name only a few. These Old Testament men and women are archetypes or prophetic shadows of New Testament apostolic leadership. We can examine their lives, circumstances, and responses to help us understand this aspect of leadership in a better light.

Delegated Authority

Legitimate authority is always delegated! Delegated authority is given, and someone else gives it. There is no such thing as a legitimate self-appointed leader. Authority cannot be taken, learned, or stumbled upon. There are those specific persons whom God has chosen to delegate this authority to. Those people, in most cases, are found serving in the church. The authorization also comes in different "shapes and sizes" if you will. Some may be authorized to use it only in the church (or to a group of churches), some may be only authorized to use it trans-locally (not in their church – but in other churches); or others may be authorized to only use it extra-locally (outside of the church entirely, say in a

business). Regardless of *where* one is authorized to use it, only those *from* the church can be authorized to use it. So there are two caveats to wielding this type of delegated authority:
- Having the authorization from someone else.
- Being a contributing member of a local church.

While the gifting may always be there... authorization (or the authority you need to use the gift to its full and intended end) can be forfeit, and it is forfeited when you break or leave covenant with the Church or a local church. The issue is never about losing the gift, it is about the authority or legitimacy of having the right to operate the gift in the sphere God has called you to use it.

It is important to distinguish between the spiritual authority of every believer and what I am calling apostolic or delegated authority. Every believer in Jesus Christ is an ambassador and has awesome power as a representative of the name and person of Jesus Christ. In no way am I diminishing the awesome power and authority of the believer to pray for the sick, take authority over spirits, discern, etc. I will not take the time to go into detail on the authority of the believer, suffices to say every believer has incredible authority in the spirit, but not every Christian is given the authority to occupy a visible and formal leadership role.

Leaders are trailblazers, decision makers and assumers of responsibility.

Definitions of Leadership

Numerous authors have published definitions or descriptions of leadership, in fact, there are thousands of published definitions. All these definitions or descriptions represent leadership to some degree, some are vague and others are extremely detailed. There are definitions as short as a five-word sentence and others as long as 25 pages (yes, one definition is actually that long). Leadership science is discovering and uncovering nuances of leadership every day that warrant more explanation. It is good that leadership is under such scrutiny, but it is also troublesome in that there is little coherence between definitions. I have chosen to include a few descriptions that I have come across, concerning leadership.

1. Warren Bennis & Burt Nanus say that "leadership is... doing the right thing."[1]
2. James McGregor Burns says, "Leadership is when persons with certain motives and purposes mobilize, in competition or conflict with others, institutional, political, psychological and other resources so as to arouse, engage and satisfy the motives of followers."[1]
3. Tom Peters says, "Leadership is mastering paradoxes and what they stand for."[8]
4. J. Oswald Sanders says, "Leadership is influence."[1]
5. Garry Willis says, "Leadership is mobilizing others toward a goal shared by the leader and followers."[1]
6. George Barna says, "A Christian leader is someone who is called by God to lead and possess virtuous character and effectively motivates, mobilizes resources, and directs people toward the fulfillment of a jointly embraced vision from God."[1]
7. Kirby Clements says, "Leaders are pathfinders who are willing to make decisions and assume responsibility for others."[2]
8. Frank Damazio says, "Vanguards [leaders] have the unique responsibility to see into the future with prophetic insight yet to be able to take the people pastorally, without discouragement, from the past into the future."[3]

Perhaps my favorite definition of leadership is from Dr. Kirby Clements (#7). His book, *The Second*, concisely sums up leaders as "trailblazers, decision makers and assumers of responsibility." All three elements of risk, decisiveness, and responsibility must be in the leader's makeup. Responsibility is one facet of leadership that is being abandoned. Apostolically-minded leaders must not abandon their sense of responsibility to the assignment or from taking responsibility for their actions. To act responsibly requires an acute understanding of the fear of the Lord. No leader can lead effectively or rule efficiently without a fear of God. Any work that is done without the fear of the Lord is in jeopardy.

It is also noteworthy that the three elements of leadership, 1) risk taking, 2) decisiveness, and 3) responsibility, alluded to in that definition cannot be attained by education and training. One is not automatically a risk taker, decisive, or even able to shoulder large amounts of responsibility. God places these qualities there, either at birth, by God's process of growth, or re-birth.

Revelation and Authority

Perhaps the greatest factor that marks an apostolically-minded leader is his authority. By exploring biblical models, we see that delegated authority hinges on revelation. Authority is a product of revelation, and revelation is the product of being a God seeker. Moses had his place of authority among the Israelites because of his revelation of God. God spoke to Moses differently than how he spoke to others. In a confrontation with Miriam and Aaron over his Cushite wife (Numbers 12), Miriam asked this question, "Does the Lord only speak through Moses?" The question offended God, so much so that He struck Miriam with leprosy (another example of the consequences of not asking the right question). The Lord's reply to Miriam was,

> "Hear now My words: If there is a prophet among you, I, the LORD, make myself known to him in a vision; I speak to him in a dream. Not so with My servant Moses; He is faithful in all My house. I speak with him face to face, even plainly, and not in dark sayings; and he sees the form of the LORD. Why then were you not afraid to speak against My servant Moses?"[4]

What God was telling Miriam was that Moses had a much higher level of revelation and insight of the things of God than his contemporaries. Moses heard God plainly and not in the riddles, which He spoke to other men. This revelation gave him a higher level of authority.

It is also apparent that similar levels of revelation worked in the lives of Abraham, Samuel, Elijah, Peter, Paul, and others, which gave them a greater authority. For example, Peter seemed to have a higher degree of authority, or at least, influence, among the twelve, especially after Jesus' ascension. I believe this was in part due to his revelation of who Jesus was. Remember that it was Peter who declared, "You are the Christ the Son of the living God," and Jesus, said, that flesh and blood did not reveal that to him.[5] Peter experienced a divine revelation of Christ that seemed to be hidden from others, and this revelation may have been a platform for his authority among the other apostles. As you will notice in our later discussion on Moses and Samuel the concept of divine revelation is woven throughout these examples and is a distinguishing characteristic of a sent leader.

5

The Leader as Shepherd

Leadership is one of the most important roles in the local church and shepherding is the model that God uses to portray leadership! I have already mentioned what Paul says in Romans 12:8 that those who have the gift of leadership should use it diligently. In other words, if you are a leader, be intentional about it and practice it with care. Later, Paul tells the young pastor, Timothy, that desiring leadership in the local church is a good or praiseworthy thing. Obviously, Paul had an affinity for making sure the most capable and gifted leaders were in the church. I can only presume, but I suppose this was because Paul believed that the members of the body of Christ should be equipped and trained in the church by the same capable leaders.

The roles of a shepherd in the local church are many and varied, and apostolically-minded leaders if not naturally gifted as a shepherd must learn to be so. However, there are also roles and functions that are distinct to shepherds. I believe those with apostolic assignments must learn to shepherd, but it is not necessarily true that shepherds become apostolic. In fact, many of the frustrations that local churches experience are because shepherds are going outside of their capacity to try and mimic the apostolic because they perceive – or have been told – that it is a higher level or more anointed position of leadership. Nothing could be further from the truth. Likewise, many churches suffer unnecessarily because the apostolically-minded leader is not dedicated to the needs of the sheep. Likewise, they can fall victim to the belief that somehow shepherding is a lesser assignment than an apostolic one.

The successful operation of the shepherd is an integral piece to the success and progress of the body of Christ. The shepherd occupies a distinct role in the ministry and function of the local church, which if left undone will result in the disorientation and scattering of the sheep. The enemy knows that if he can remove the shepherd or render the shepherd useless then he has won a victory. The scriptures are full of examples of sheep who were scattered because there was no shepherd to lead, guide, and protect them (I Kings 22:17; Zechariah 13:7). This is another reason why I believe that pastorally-minded leaders belong in the church and not in the marketplace. Because when they are not functioning in the church their gifting and passion cannot be maximized in the context where God intended them to be of the greatest value. The role of the shepherd becomes absolutely vital to the success of the church. Without a shepherd there is no tangible advancement or cohesiveness for the people of God.

Key reflection questions

1. Do you have a desire to lead?
2. What does it mean to lead with "diligence?"

3. What have you observed about local church leaders that impress you about their calling?

Defining the role of shepherd

Before any further discussion it is essential to describe our context. Since our modern culture does not employ real shepherds the metaphor may be difficult to understand. What exactly is a shepherd and what do they do? Today, in our modern culture, the word shepherd is rendered "pastor." Contemporary pastors are often the CEO of a local church or churches. In some cases this is definitely true, but all pastors are not categorically executive leaders. Some pastors relish the role of CEO and to others it grates against their spiritual DNA. Many pastors are forced into executive positions – and I understand and have no quarrel with those who are – however, the metaphor of a shepherd is difficult to reconcile with CEO. Shepherds are intrinsically stewards and caregivers, not executive decision-makers.

Because of our modern understanding of a "pastor's" leadership role many churches and people are confused when they begin to understand the role and duties of a biblical shepherd. A shepherd certainly is a leader, but their leadership style and traits often manifest differently than one might suspect. Instead of the administrative, executive, or visionary type leader shepherds act more as protectors, nurturers, and caregivers. Biblical shepherds lead by example and lifestyle; and are constantly available and open to the sheep. This is not to say that the two types of leaders (i.e., executive leaders and shepherds) are totally irreconcilable. Many visionary leaders are also shepherds and vice-versa, but usually if one person must assume both roles, one of the aspects is a learned trait.

In the New Testament the Greek word shepherd is transliterated *poimen* and is used interchangeably with the terms pastor or elder. This is an important point. In other words, pastor and elder are synonymous, there is no distinction between them in the New Testament.

The descriptive term shepherd is a better picture of what the word *pastor* truly means. To be a pastor implies an action, it implies a demonstrated behavior, it is not an office held. Shepherds do the work of shepherding, which is to care for, feed, protect and direct the flock. The term shepherd is a much more accurate depiction of what a pastor is to do. You can think of it as the term "pastor" being a job title and the term "shepherd" as the job description. Therefore, it is important not confuse the issue by categorically assuming that every leader in a church has a shepherd's heart or a shepherd's motivation. Often the leader or leaders we call "pastor" is a description of the office they hold and not a description of their ministry, gift, or motivation.

The shepherd is not like other leaders, who lead because of a title or office, but shepherds lead because of their relationship with people.

Having said that, it is important to clarify that many senior leaders of churches definitely have a true shepherd's heart, In fact all elders must be able to shepherd the people of God (I Peter 5:2), regardless of what they believe about their ministry, gift, or calling. Any and all elders in the local church must be shepherds to the flock that God has placed them in. Because shepherding is also a job, and not only a calling or gift, many of the skills of a shepherd can be learned and perfected. This fact is also supported by Paul's description to Timothy concerning who can be an elder. If you consult Paul's list of qualifications of an elder you will find that very few – if any – are gifts, per se. Most are elements of discipline and character.

The Hebrew word for shepherd is *ra'ah* and gives us a little better look at what a shepherd is and does; it means to tend a flock, to rule, keep company with, or to make friendship with. It is implied in this definition of a shepherd that any ruling aspect of shepherding is demonstrated in conjunction with an established relationship.

This aspect of relating poses a very interesting caveat to the role of the shepherd. The shepherd is not like other leaders, who lead because of a title or office, but shepherds lead because of their relationship with the people (see Matthew 20:25-26). By this definition a shepherd cannot have authority in another flock because there is no relationship there. The authority of the shepherd is not based on title or office, but it is a relational-based authority that is given by the people after trust is earned. Therefore, one of the dominant concepts of shepherding is relationship. There is no shepherd who can have success in ministry without relationship. So here we find one distinction, an apostle's authority is rooted in revelation, and a shepherd's authority is rooted in relationship. Shepherds can have revelation and apostles can have relationship, but one is usually dominant.

What does having relationship mean? Simply that people – and not money, title, or positions – are the reason pastors do what they do. That may be a bit overstated, but suffice it to say elders and pastors who want to be effective shepherds like to be around and in constant contact with people.

Jesus: the ultimate Shepherd

Jesus is the ultimate fulfillment of the shepherd. This is not to say there are no good shepherds today, but only that The Shepherd has come and shown us what a perfect shepherd is like and what he does (John 10). To look at what Jesus did is to know what a shepherd is to do.

Psalm 23 gives a very clear portrait of the Lord, as our ultimate Shepherd. By examining this passage shepherds today can see what it is they are to do. There is not time to outline every element of Jesus' shepherding, so we will only discuss a few. Verse one of chapter 23 declares His authority and role, "The Lord is my shepherd" David voluntarily submits to the Lord's leading. Sheep today will validate your ministry by following you based on your track record and relationship.

Obviously, shepherds are not shepherds if they have no sheep. An old adage says, "He who thinks he is leading and has no one following him is only out for a walk." King David is declaring himself a follower by acknowledging the Lord as his shepherd. The irony here is that David himself was a pretty good shepherd. There are many accounts of him saving his father's sheep's from lions and bears – so we know that David knew how to protect sheep. Yet, in a true shepherd's fashion David submits to a greater shepherd. Showing us the best way to get followers is to be a follower.

The second statement of verse 1 of Psalm 23 is, "I shall not want." What a potent declaration. This is the ultimate picture that all shepherds should subscribe to, and that picture is, With Him as Shepherd there is no lack. The Lord can supply all our needs and in Him there is no want. Today earthly shepherds cannot meet every need, but they can meet some. Even the apostle Paul promotes the notion of meeting other's needs.

> [19]*For though I am free from all men, I have made myself a servant to all, that I might win the more;* [20]*and to the Jews I became as a Jew, that I might win Jews;*

> to those who are under the law, as under the law, that I might win those who are under the law; ^{21}to those who are without law, as without law (not being without law toward God, but under law toward Christ), that I might win those who are without law; ^{22}to the weak I became as weak, that I might win the weak. I have become all things to all men that I might by all means save some. ^{23}Now this I do for the gospel's sake, that I may be partaker of it with you. (I Corinthians 9:19-22)

As shepherds in the house of God we should do our best to meet the needs of those God has placed under our care. Moses modeled for us (Exodus 18:21-22) that each elder has a different capacity to lead. Do not despise your capacity. Some have the grace to lead 10, some 50, some 100, and some 1000, but no matter your leadership capacity all shepherds must meet the same eligibility requirements.

This necessity to satisfy the same requirements can become a point of contention for some shepherds. Shepherds must guard their heart carefully to not become envious of another shepherd's portion (i.e., gifting, sphere of authority, or talent) even though they are asked to fulfill the same qualifications. As humans it is easy for us to misconstrue what we think is fair or owed to us. We inherently believe that because we meet some predetermined standard or criteria that we are entitled to the same benefits and courtesies as our peers. This is one of those differences I referred to in an earlier chapter about the differences between church-based leadership and contemporary business or organizational models of leadership. Concepts like seniority and equality have different meanings in a family versus a business. Each of the shepherds picked in Exodus 18 were required to satisfy the same qualifications, but – based on their grace – some were given 1,000 to rule over and others only ten. This principle is also clearly depicted in the New Testament (1 Corinthians 12) when Paul describes that there are different administrations and distributions of the same gifts. In other words, shepherds – as all believers – must guard their heart from gift envy.

What other models does the Lord provide for us in Psalm 23?
1. Makes me lie down (in green pastures) – implies dealing with stubbornness
2. Leads me (beside still water) – implies being an example of calm and contentment
3. Restores my soul
4. Leads me (in the path of righteousness) – implies a lifestyle of righteousness
5. Removes fear no evil
6. He is with us
7. Comforts (with rod and staff)
8. Prepares a table before my enemies
9. Anoints us
10. Goodness and mercy follow me

Let's briefly summarize each of the following statements as a short-of job description for the pastoral leader.

These are obviously oversimplified, but "He makes me lie down in green pastures," "leads me by still waters," and "restores my soul" can all speak of the shepherd's ability to bring peace and rest. Shepherds must model to their flock peacefulness; and be able to help calm the storms, chaos, and crisis of life. How this is done varies from shepherd to shepherd, it may be counsel, it may be weeping together, laughing together, just being there, but a shepherd will help quiet the busyness and chaos of the heart. Another key is the picture of leading. Jesus very definitely leads us.

So shepherds also must lead. Shepherds must know how to get to the "green pastures" and "still water."

Jesus our Shepherd also, "leads us in paths of righteousness" which speaks of his example to us. A shepherd must live a life that can stand up under scrutiny. Character and integrity are vital to success as a shepherd. Gifting and talent will never hold open any doors that are shut by a lack of character or integrity. The "rod and staff" that bring comfort speak of the boundaries that are set. One of the ways a shepherd will protect his flock is by placing boundaries around them. A wise shepherd will let his flock have all the freedom they desire and imagination and creativity they can muster as long as they do not put themselves in harm's way by going outside of the safe boundaries. A good Shepherd also knows when to expand the boundaries for certain sheep when necessary.

A good shepherd will anoint his flock. The Hebrew context of this statement is about healing and medicine. Shepherds would literally pour oil on the head of the sheep to keep the flies away, which again deals with the idea that a shepherd protects and heals their flock. Not only is the shepherd a source of healing and protection, but true shepherds have their own bottle of oil, which is a symbol of the Holy Spirit and represents divine anointing.

This look at Psalm 23 was cursory and in no way was meant to be exhaustive. The picture of Jesus and portrait of a shepherd presented here is awesome. Any elder or pastor should meditate on this portion of scripture in detail, so as to get a clear picture of what a shepherd should be like.

Lastly, remember the Lord's commission to Peter when He restored him in John chapter 21. He told Peter to "feed my lambs." Once more we see this essential task of the shepherd's role to feed taking center stage! I encourage you to keep in mind that although we have described the role of a shepherd that all apostolically-minded leaders, despite the unique calling, still must embrace a shepherd's responsibilities.

6

What Shepherds Do Best

Let me remind you that all leaders must shepherd (pastor), but not all shepherds are (or need to be) leaders. There are plenty of shepherds (pastors) in the body of Christ who are providing excellent care for the sheep yet have no formal leadership titles or roles. On the other hand, there are also many official leaders (apostolic or otherwise) who do have formal leadership roles and titles, but are not nurturing the sheep. Therefore, it is important to tell leaders, especially those with an apostolic assignment what it is that shepherds do, because they more than others are prone to forget that shepherding is a prerequisite for their assignment.

Building relationships

Developing and maintaining relationships are major concerns that shepherds must deal with. There are practical duties that shepherds can do to foster and create relationships. One is to spend time with people. Time is one of the greatest assets a shepherd can give to people. In fact, it is how well that time is spent that makes or breaks the shepherd. Often people will evaluate your worth as a pastor, based on how much attention or time they perceive you give them. If there is a high perception of time and attention given, then people will tend to value you more highly as a pastor and validate your leadership. If they perceive that you do not give much time or attention they are not as likely to validate your leadership.

Shepherds must be people-oriented, completing a task has its place, but do not displace people to accomplish a task. Sometimes the apostolically-minder leader does not follow this rule of thumb. The reverse side of that coin is shepherds must also administrate, focusing on people disproportionately can also cause failures in other areas of leadership. But the priority most certainly should be on the people.

The first shepherd: Tending and keeping

The Old and New Testaments have a lot to say about the duties and requirements for shepherds. I want to focus on what the Old Testament says about the requirements and functions of the shepherd.

The very first mention of a shepherd in the Bible is Adam. Adam was given a charge to "tend and keep" the Garden of Eden, which included among other duties being a literal shepherd. Part of his tending and keeping included watching over and naming the animals. To tend and to keep, is a major role the shepherd must accept. "To tend" is the Hebrew word *awbad* and it means "to work, bring to pass, or husbandman." This implies a great deal of responsibility on the part of the one who is to tend. Even before tilling the ground was necessary to sustain life Adam was charged to tend and keep the garden. Perhaps what is more significant is that the word *awbad* carries the connotation of worship and is translated five times in the Old Testament as "worshippers." For Adam tending to the garden involved worship, and worship is service. The shepherd must never lose the heart of a worshiping servant. There is no room for self-serving shepherds the body of Christ.

To "keep" the garden is also a critical aspect of the shepherd's role. As a keeper of the garden, Adam was its steward or manager. The Hebrew word "keep" is *shawmar* and means "to hedge about, protect and take heed to self." This is an awesome thing for the pastorally-minded leaders of today. Shepherds in all their duties as rulers, subduers, and worshippers are also to add to their list protectors. Shepherds are in fact protectors of what God has placed under their care. What they are protecting are usually people and geographical regions. But they also must protect their own hearts, their own actions, and their own motives. The shepherd must take heed to him or herself, being careful not to abuse their God-given authority or influence. As with all stewards, there will be a day when every shepherd will have to give account for what they have done with God's people.

The parable of the talents obviously comes to mind – will God reward you with leadership over even more cities, or will He take yours away and give it to someone else? Shepherds must help people grow and excel. Shepherds must avoid the temptation of secluding their flock in the guise of "protection" thus becoming like the evil servant who buried his talent.

Shepherd as feeder

Genesis 46:32 is not the first reference to shepherds in the Bible, but it is the first one with a job description assigned to it, it says, "the men are shepherds, for their occupation has been to feed livestock." This is extremely significant. The shepherd is a feeder of the flock. A shepherd without food is no shepherd.

To feed something implies giving and sustaining life. There can be no life and certainly no health if there is no nutrition. The Merriam-Webster dictionary's definition of the verb *feed* is "to give food, and to provide something essential to the growth." Providing what is essential for growth is truly the crux of shepherding. Therefore, a wise shepherd "weeds out" the dangerous food before serving the sheep.

No shepherd can escape the feeding aspect of their ministry. One may ask, what food do I give? The answer is whatever is essential for their growth. In other words, there is no preset formula. All sheep are different and require different food based on the season of life they are in. Keep in mind that what is nutritious and causes one to grow may not cause the other to grow. For example, mother's milk has no value for a mature adult, but is essential for an infant. Likewise, meat can be harmful to an infant, but valuable to those who are full grown. It is the pastor who must discern which food is essential for growth for each person they are charged to care for.

Imagine only giving a teenage boy baby formula and asking them to perform well in school or at a sporting event. This is one reason why, as we mentioned before, relationship is so important.

How will a shepherd know what is essential, unless there is adequate time involved in learning the habits and needs of the sheep? Jesus modeled this for us perfectly, with one disciple, He acted and said certain things a certain way, yet with another disciple He might have responded completely different. Feeding is one of the most important functions a shepherd performs in their daily duties.

An examination of Jeremiah 3:15 reveals a little more to us about the "feeding" roles of a shepherd. The Lord says that He will give us (i.e., His people) shepherds who feed us knowledge and understanding. All shepherds must be able to give knowledge and understanding as part of the food they pass out. A shepherd who cannot feed is worthless. That is not to say if you are not a talented or gifted speaker or teacher you cannot be an excellent shepherd, you most certainly can be. Many shepherds are excellent "teachers" one-on-one or in small groups and may not be as prolific in larger groups or different settings. That is perfectly okay. Paul in his letter to Timothy says that anyone who desires to be a leader in the local church must be "apt to teach." This implies to be *ready* or *fit* to instruct and not presume mastery or expert ability.

One last note; Ezekiel 34:2 gives a tremendous condemnation against the shepherds of Israel for not feeding the flock. The Lord says, "Woe to the shepherds of Israel who feed themselves! Should not the shepherds feed the flock?" Obviously, God takes this matter of feeding the sheep very seriously. Shepherd who get into leadership positions because of what the title or position offers are in grave danger of "feeding themselves," something which the Lord hates.

Shepherd as leader

Numbers 27:17 gives us insight into the shepherd's broad range of leadership abilities. Moses asked the Lord to provide shepherds for the people who would lead them out and lead them in. Leading them *out* is a reference to moving ahead when it is necessary; leading them *in* is a reference to returning home when necessary. In essence, Moses is asking for shepherds who can help him get the people ready to advance ahead when necessary, stay in one place when the people want to leave prematurely, and help the people return home when they lose their way.

Sheep have to have someone to follow. It is clear by this passage that Moses is implying people without a shepherd do not move. This is another reason why the shepherd's role is vital. They must get the people to move, left to their own often times people will stay in one place, eat all the grass, drink all the water, sit still, and eventually die. A shepherd is always looking for fresh water, better food, richer sources of nutrition, and greater heights. Without shepherds, many people will be content with where they are and contentment with the status quo is equivalent to death.

Shepherd as ruler

There is no doubt that there is a clear rulership aspect to shepherding, but as stated earlier, the right to rule comes by relating, befriending, feeding; it is not granted as part of a title or office. Samuel was an example of a shepherd who ruled. The Lord said to him plainly, "you shall shepherd my people, and be ruler over Israel" (II Samuel 7:2, I Chronicles 11:2). The Lord implied in his command to Samuel that shepherding is ruling and ruling is shepherding, but He also implies a divine difference. The difference is seen in that he tells Samuel to shepherd *and* be a ruler. It is subtle but none-the-less it is there, the two roles have different mentalities and a wise shepherd will know when to wear the shepherd's hat and when to wear the ruler's hat. For a true pastorally-minded leader, having to pull rank in order to accomplish a goal breaks their heart.

The gentle shepherd

Because of the necessity to rule and propensity in man's heart to take advantage of ruling, there is also a very necessary nurturing and caregiving side to the shepherd. Isaiah 40:11 lists four things a shepherd does. One, he feeds his flock. Two, gathers the lambs. Three, carries them in his bosom. And, four, gently leads. This is an obvious declaration of the gentleness required of a shepherd. Think about how a shepherd would carry lambs in his bosom. This is a process obviously requiring patience, skill, precision, and grace. This depiction of the shepherd is awesome. All shepherds must have a nurturing side to their ministry. Not every sheep is strong and healthy. In fact, many are weak, hurting, and young. It is with these sheep shepherds must take extra care by being gentile. Hold them close to your bosom, share intimate times with them, laugh when they laugh, and cry when they cry. A shepherd who is gentle is a good shepherd. Think about the Lord and how He shepherds us (Psalm 23). We all need a tender touch from time to time!

What a shepherd does not do

There are many accounts of God warning or punishing Israel's shepherds for doing certain things deemed "unshepherdlike." For instance Isaiah 56:11, "they are shepherds who cannot understand; they all look to their own way, everyone for his own gain."

This is a stern warning to the shepherd who has no understanding or discretion. Wisdom and understanding are high commodities to the Lord. Proverbs tells us plainly to seek wisdom (Proverbs 2:1-5). The Bible admonishes us to seek wisdom and understanding from the Lord; if we do He promises to give it to us (James 1:5). But shepherds who are not interested in learning (i.e., are unteachable) have no business being shepherds and should be expelled from their role by other trust-worthy shepherds.

Shepherds who only look out for themselves and have no interest in guarding or protecting the sheep have only trouble ahead of them. Jesus Himself our ultimate shepherd sits at the door of the sheepfold protecting us (John 10:1-17) we too must follow His example.

Jeremiah 10:21 declares that the Lord will scatter the sheep of shepherds who have become "dull-hearted" and "have not sought the Lord." What an indictment. Having your sheep scatter at the hand of God is a terrible thing. It is fair to assume that being discredited by God is a hard thing to recover from. Therefore, learn from Jeremiah 10 and take heed to purposefully seek the Lord and remain sensitive of heart.

Shepherds must keep alert and attentive to the leading and guiding of the Holy Spirit. Jeremiah 50:6 depicts the Lord's anger with the shepherds because they went "from mountain to hill." These shepherds actually took their sheep from a high place to a low place. What a tragedy. The Lord desires that shepherds take the sheep up to the mountain because the mountain is where the Lord dwells. As shepherds, we must follow and pursue the Lord, not our own agendas or plans. Jeremiah, Ezekiel, and Zechariah all go on in several other passages that condemn shepherds for "feeding themselves," driving the sheep away, scattering His flock, not attending to the sheep's needs, not being their physician, leaving the flock outright, and not pitying the sheep. Nahum speaks of the "slumbering shepherds." God takes His sheep and their care very seriously so too must shepherds! Remember – as cliché as it is – shepherds are in the sheep business.

Part 2

Wherever you send us we will go. Joshua 1:16b

Introduction to Part 2

In this section, we are going to take a departure from pastoral and apostolic forms of leadership. Now, I want to talk exclusively about the Old Testament leaders who stood out in a crowd and had an apostolic assignment. I am excited about this section because it is extremely practical and will give you specific insight and action steps. Each chapter is about a different Old Testament leader; and outlines different aspects of why I believe they were sent. While they were not apostles in a technical sense, these Old Testament leaders serve as powerful examples of sent leaders.

I hope that you will gain a new appreciation for the kind of dedication and discipline God looks for from those He sends. You'll find that often times God allows you to be trained and equipped in one setting, then pulls you out of that setting, makes you unlearn everything you learned, then requires you to relearn everything you thought you already knew. He often does that so you can be effective to the people that He sends you to. I have come to believe that God's format for leadership development requires us to learn to embrace ambiguity and become comfortable with chaos. Chaos has never meant what it has become to be associated with, disorder and confusion, in actuality chaos is merely an unrecognized or non-linear pattern. Ironically, this is exactly how God develops many of His leaders. You will see in the following chapters how God uses ambiguous and often chaotic processes to refine and develop His leaders.

7

Apostolic Assignment of Adam

Adam was history's very first apostolic prototype. Arguably there may be no greater foreshadow of apostolic leadership in the Old Testament than Adam. Adam's responsibilities in the garden were and are exactly the same responsibilities that apostolic leaders have today. By looking into Adam's responsibilities, behaviors, and relationships we can learn a great deal about what and how God intended delegated authority to do and be.

Adam's relationship with God was unique. No other human has before or since related to God the way that Adam was able to relate to God. At least for a season of time, Adam had a perfect, unhindered relationship with the God. Adam's reflection of God was perfect; he was genetically engineered by God, with DNA that was unmarred and untouched by sin. He was not birthed into sin, like the rest of mankind since. At least for a short season, there was no sin to confound or confuse his spiritual senses. Adam experienced God the Creator unhindered. Adam's initial relationship with God combined with the fact that God delegated to him face-to-face, unparalleled authority, which allows us to see what God intended a true apostolic assignment to be like.

Today, because of sin our authority is limited to certain spheres and constrained by time. Adam's original authority contained no boundaries and was not restricted by time. This small insight into what God's original intent might have been for men and women as we work in the world is profound. He intended us to have dominion and rule in every sphere and every place we were sent to. However, once sin was introduced into the garden Adam's domain shrunk and was now restricted to a sphere with guarded boundaries. We today can still function on the earth with incredible God-delegated levels of authority and power, but typically that authority is confined to a specific sphere. Therefore, it is essential we, as Christians, learn to hear God's voice and understand our intended purpose so that we can find that sphere and thrive in it.

Adam had authority as a direct result of two key dynamics:
1. God sending him
2. His revelation of God (note: we will see this as a recurring theme of apostolic leaders)

Adam's sentness

God sent the first Adam, just as He sent the last Adam (Jesus); both were sent by God, and both understood that if God's plan were to be realized on the earth it would not be by their own authority, but rather the authority of The Sender (John 7:16,29). In fact, our perfect model of an apostolically-minded leader, Jesus, said that the authority that He operated in was not His own.[1] Jesus' authority was in fact "on loan." One of the key premises of authority, in terms of being sent, is that all authority ultimately belongs to the sender and is never truly "owned" by the receiver. Unlike spiritual gifts, authority can be given and taken away.

Leaders who are sent are agents acting on behalf of the one who sent them. This is so much the case in apostolic leadership that those who receive the one sent are receiving the sender (John 13:20; I Corinthians 4:17). In fact, we can say that the one who is sent, is, in essence, unified with the sender; to receive the first is to receive the second. This is the reason why such great discernment must go into the calling, releasing, and sending of leaders.

There is a three step process toward the full functioning of delegated authority. The three-steps are:

1. The calling
2. The releasing
3. The sending

God calls, then there is a recognition of that call (first by the individual then by others). After others recognize the call there comes a release. The release is to perform the duties and function in that authority within a predefined scope or context, which is what happens after you recognize your assignment. After the release, there is an additional development stage, which may (or may not) be followed by being sent into a larger sphere. Sometimes that larger sphere is a removal of constraints within your existing sphere, other times it means going into new territory. It is important to note that it is possible to be released into ministry but never be sent. The third stage of being sent is a divine prerogative, and is not a prerequisite for effective ministry, but it is necessary for apostolic authority.

Once sent, it is important to understand that there are two levels of authority to represent: 1) the natural, and 2) the divine. The natural refers to the human agency that did the literal sending (e.g., elders). The divine is God. It would do all of us well to consider and remember that all authority while having come from God, is recognized and conferred by people. Therefore, at no time is anyone excused from the obligation to represent their "sender," both in the natural and divine. We represent our natural authority by doing our job with excellence and exceeding expectations of those around us. We represent the divine by having the mind of Christ in all things, being submitted to authority, exceeding any ethical and all integrity expectations, and remembering our resources come from God and not man.

Authority is a direct result of revelation.

Ultimately all authority belongs to God[2]; it is His to disseminate as He sees fit. However, this is not an excuse to bypass or disregard the process established by men and women to govern those they send. Nothing that any "sent one" can do can increase their authority unless God gives it and man recognizes it. This is the great mystery of delegated authority – it is a paradox – recognition of any authority no matter how divine must be appreciated by the people to whom one is sent. Remember, there is no such thing as self-sending. In fact, few things are more distasteful to people than a self-appointed leader, especially one who calls himself or herself an apostle. A self-appointed apostle is an oxymoron and a contradiction of terms.

Man can increase in influence, ability, learn new behaviors, acquire traits and skills, and many other attributes pertaining to leadership, but ultimately, authority is given. Even power can be stolen or taken, but authority is always conferred, it is always delegated. Authority is given by God and recognized by man. Without the recognition of that authority by man, any dimension of authority will be limited.

Adam's revelation of God

Adam also had divine communion with God. Adam had a revelation of God comparable only to Jesus' revelation of His Father. The revelation of God that Adam had qualified him to operate in the authority necessary to subdue the earth. Authority is a direct result of revelation. Because of his revelation of God, that is his view of God without the veil of sinful flesh, he was uniquely qualified to rule (have dominion and subdue) the earth. Once Adam and his equal partner, Eve, had accomplished dominion upon the earth they would have had the ability to rule justly. I believe God would have allowed Adam to rule supremely over the earth as His representative, God would have had total confidence in Adam's ability to rule as His appointed delegate.

The very fact that God Almighty was willing to let man represent Him on the earth is a sobering reality of the intensity of the grace and mercy of God. Jesus, the last Adam, stated that, "My judgment is true; for I am not alone, but I am one with the Father who sent Me" (John 8:16 NKJV). Before the fall of man, this too was the human race's quest – to make perfect judgments, just as the Father would. This ability to judge rightly can only come as a result of the revelation of God and is part of what makes the apostolically-minded leader unique.

The first apostolic mandate

As the first leader sent to the earth, Adam was given special commands or duties, I call these, apostolic mandates. The first apostolic mandates that were given to Adam can serve as a model for all apostolically-minded leaders today:

1. Be fruitful
2. Multiply
3. Fill the earth
4. Subdue the earth
5. Have dominion
6. Tend and keep the garden
7. Name all the animals

These mandates should be applied to our practice of leadership today. Without a clear picture of what these things mean and symbolize, it will be difficult to operate as a sent leader.

Be fruitful, multiply and fill the earth

The command to be fruitful and multiply (Genesis 1:28) is more than a command to procreate. The deeper implication is to produce fruit; more importantly, to produce life. Any leader should leave an abundance of life in their wake as they minister and go from place to place. Sent leaders, by their nature, should be ones who command a greater performance from the lives of those they were sent to lead. The production of "greater life" should be a by-product of their energy and vision. This is demonstrated by Jesus Himself, who said that, "I came so that you could have life, and life more abundantly."[3]

As a human, and as a result of sin, we have a predisposition to negativity. When faced with any form of confrontation, many people will flee. It is the natural flight-or-fight response to stress that all humans share. Part of the filling the earth mandate is an abandonment of your fleeing response. If indeed God has sent you then the option of "flight" or fleeing is not available. The delegated leader must operate out the mindset of "filling the earth," and the earth will not be filled if confrontation always results in you fleeing away. As a delegated leader God will give the grace and passion for continuing in the face of adversity to accomplish His purpose. Paul disciplined himself and pressed on toward the high mark, Jesus faced adversity and did not flee from it and as a result of His defeating death we can experience greater life today!

Subdue and have dominion

The Garden of Eden was under attack; the presence of Satan in the garden is evidence of that. When we examine the words used in the Hebrew for dominion and subdue, *radah* and *kawash*, they mean to subjugate, tread down, dominate, scrape out, conquer, violate, or bring into subjection.[4]

God was telling Adam that because he was God's representative he would be involved in violence. Satan was seeking to rob, steal, and destroy anything he could from Adam, and eventually stole his authority and government. For Adam to defeat the enemy, he would need to be violent toward the enemy. Sent leaders cannot be passive – there must be an active strategy at work to keep the momentum moving forward.

The irony is of course that delegated authority results in violence that is intended to "make peace." This is not a natural peace, the kind that you experience by sitting next to a babbling brook on a cool summer day, but the supernatural peace of God's Kingdom that is beyond understanding (Philippians 4:7), but not beyond experience.

Divinely delegated leadership represents God's peace and breaks the yoke of the enemy; it involves the destroying of principalities and powers. Just as there are other ministries to break other yokes – for example, the prophetic breaks the yoke of discouragement, teaching breaks the yoke of ignorance – so too apostolic leadership breaks a specific yoke. Apostolic leaders break the yolk of oppression. Whenever Paul and his apostolic team entered a city it seemed an uproar of some kind would occur. Why, because there was a disturbance among the spiritual rulers and principalities of the city. Why, because true apostolic leadership is the only legitimate government with God's seal and authority to rule over a region. This reality is offensive to a hostile occupying force.

Tending and keeping

To *tend and keep* are two additional functions of apostolic leadership that we see evident in Adam's life. To tend is the Hebrew word *awbad*. It means to work, bring to pass, or husbandman.[6] This is, in fact, nothing less than servanthood. It implies a great deal of responsibility on the part of the one who is to tend. Even before Adam was cursed to till the ground for food he still had to tend the land. Why? Because the Hebrew understanding of tending implied more than cultivating, it has also been interpreted as worship. For Adam (and for us) tending to the land is a command to worship, which requires tending to our heart and attitude. We accomplish that by working with excellence.

"To keep" the garden is also key to delegated leadership. As a keeper of the garden, Adam was its steward or manager. The Hebrew word keep is *shawmar*. It means to hedge about, protect and take heed to self.[7] In the chapter on shepherding we discussed the unique responsibility and privilege of what it means for a leader to protect. But now I would like to focus on the aspect of "to keep" that addresses taking heed to self.

One of the things that needs to be protected – perhaps most of all – is the heart, desires, and motives of the leader. To keep the garden is a clear command to guard your heart. Apostolic leaders are to take heed to themselves, being careful not to abuse their God-given authority or influence.

Lastly, "to tend and keep the garden" implies a geographic domain. Adam had charge only over the garden. Note that this is not a contradiction to what I mentioned earlier in this chapter about Adams authority not having boundaries. Remember part of Adam's original mandate was to subdue the earth. Adam base of operation was from the garden, with the expectation that he expand that garden as far as he could expand it. So, while boundaries were in place, I believe it was God's intention that those boundaries be transient. In other words, Adam had the permission to expand those boundaries as far as he liked. Unfortunately, by disobeying God's command, he not only forfeited his flexible and fluid boundaries, but also his original base of operation.

Even before Adam was cursed to till the ground for food he still had to tend the land.

In fact, when he was expelled from the garden, Adam lost all authority he once had. No longer was he able to rule; he now became a slave to the earth and had to serve it. This is an important lesson also modeled for us by Paul's ministry. Paul refused to build on another man's foundation and stated that there were spheres of authority.[8] As long as delegated leaders stay within their sphere, and do not promote or send themselves out they will have God's grace and favor to establish government and rule, but if that integrity is violated then the covering and safety net of the authority is forfeit.

Giving a name

Naming the animals is an important demonstration of how to use delegated authority. This responsibility calls for a high level of revelation and discernment. The ultimate fate and future of every living creature resided in what Adam decided their name should be. It was delegated to Adam to assign identity, roles, meaning and purpose. Whatever Adam said they were is what they became. The implication of giving a name implies defining boundaries, setting into motion attitudes and behaviors, and creating identity. This is a responsibility that someone who is sent takes seriously and is a function of an apostolic assignment. This kind of authority and revelation ought to be embedded deep in the DNA of the delegated leader. The kind of authority to give identity to something or someone requires careful guarding and intense sense of awe before God.

Adam's failure

In spite of Adam's huge advantage (i.e., a sinless birth and open communication with God) he still failed. This should serve as a poignant example of the fallibility of man – no matter how great the calling, perfect the environment, anointed the ministry, or talented the leader, man is nothing without a proper relationship with God. Therefore, the highest priority of any Christian leader regardless of the model (i.e. pastoral, apostolic, or other) should be on maintaining a proper and right relationship with God. Adam's downfall can be related to two key relational weaknesses, that we would do well to consider:

1. A poor sense of self
2. Failure to properly relate those around him

Ultimately, Adam was weak and only concerned about himself, contrary to traditional anecdotes the failure in the garden was not primarily Eve's fault. Eve was not the weak one! Adam failed in his responsibility to "tend and keep" the garden. His failure caused him to become self-focused, which dramatically altered his destiny. Because Adam did not see clearly he did not stand up for what he knew to be right. He failed in the most fundamental of leadership tasks – doing the right thing.

Adam's second failure was not recognizing the grace and calling on the people around him. Unfortunately, Eve has taken the brunt of the blame for what happened in the garden that fateful day, while Eve certainly does share in the responsibility, I believe her failure may have been redeemed if Adam had honored her the way God intended. In its most basic form Adam failed to operate as a team!

Delegated leaders and those who have authority must keep themselves surrounded by others who will keep them accountable. Eve did not hold him accountable and that is where her blame lies. Adam allowed Eve to become something less than his equal companion. In doing so, Adam failed to recognize her God-given authority in his life. Adam's failure to recognize her calling by not releasing her into that place as an equal partner left her unfulfilled and as a consequence pushed her to find a counterfeit expression of her identity. This put Eve in a place of frustration over her calling and was consequently wooed by the enemy. Satan offered her want she truly wanted, equal authority, something Adam was supposed to share with her, but he failed her and as a result of Adam's unwillingness to share and Eve's impatience, both of them experienced God's judgment.

Adam failed in his relationship to Eve, which symbolically represents his peers and those he was sent to lead. Yes, a leader's relationship with God is the most important aspect and one must keep that relationship sharp and intimate. However, that is no excuse to dismiss or ignore the necessity to keep in right relationship with the people around you. I believe if Adam had properly fostered the relationship with those around him (in this case, his wife) he may have been able to redeem the situation, even after she failed.

Greatness of God

The greatness of God is also seen in the life of Adam. Adam was raised out of the ground by the supernatural breath of God as a full grown adult man. Adam needed no development, no time to mature or grow, he was complete when God created him – and by-the-way so was Eve. When both of them arrived on the scene they arrived as fully grown. Their lives were to be a testimony to others of God's capacity to create and sustain life. God created Adam – a complete person – out of the dust on the ground. They walked the earth as the crowning and ultimate symbol of God's unrestricted creative power. So too apostolic leaders are expected to reflect in their words, deeds, and action the greatness of God's unrestricted creative power by contributing early and often in new situations. This does not mean Christians do not get a learning curve, but it does mean Christians should be the first to respond and do well when in new situations.

Adam failed in his apostolic assignment and set in motion the law of sin and death for the rest of mankind. However, in His ultimate greatness, God set in motion a plan that would destroy the works of the enemy and still allow mankind the opportunity to rule and reign alongside Him.

There was another man that was raised from the ground and given supernatural life from the Father, this man was referred to as the last Adam.[9] That man is Jesus Christ, the ultimate expression of delegated authority and apostolic leadership. Jesus is the One sent to the world to redeem and repair the breach between God and man that the first Adam created. Through this last Adam mankind has been given a second chance to walk in the commissioning and fulfill the apostolic assignment given by God to the first Adam.

Because of Jesus all of us now have the capacity to fulfill the apostolic assignment given to Adam in the garden. We can fulfill the apostolic mandate and multiply, subdue and have dominion over the earth. God would not allow His plan to go unfulfilled, nor leave man without any hope of fulfilling His will on the earth. Jesus, as the last Adam, took dominion over the earth, multiplied His disciples, who later it was said "turned the world upside down," and subdued His enemies.

In His ultimate act of dominion, Jesus' victory over death itself showed His unyielding greatness and the pinnacle of authority. His immortality is a testimony of what the first Adam's life was to be in the garden a perfect existence, in perfect communion with God the Father, which we can now partake of through Jesus. The delegated authority and apostolic assignment, which was God's intent for man from the beginning, was lost. However, because of God's great grace and mercy He sent to us another way, a more perfect way for which to obtain the authority he intended for us from the beginning. That way is only through Jesus Christ.

8

Apostolic Assignment of Joseph

But now, do not therefore be grieved or angry with yourselves because you sold me here; for God sent me before you to preserve life. And God sent me before you to preserve a posterity for you in the earth, and to save your lives by a great deliverance. So now it was not you who sent me here, but God...
Genesis 45:5,7,8

The amazing story of how Joseph's apostolic assignment unfolded is told in Genesis chapters 37-50. It seems that almost everything Joseph did serves as a lesson for us about the process of delegated authority. As we see in Genesis 45 Joseph declared that it was God that sent him. I find it interesting that it took Joseph so long to realize that it was God and not his brothers who sent him to Egypt.[1] This can serve as an important reminder of how distracting the leadership journey is. In fact, it is likely that Joseph never even realized the assignment that he was on until it was nearly over. Likewise, your purpose does not have to be clearly understood before you can do something useful. Many times it is during the process of surviving that we find our path and meaning. Purpose is powerful, but sometimes we do ourselves a huge disservice by believing we must have our purpose clearly defined before we begin something, and that keeps many people from doing anything.

> *We do ourselves a huge disservice by believing we must have our purpose clearly defined before we begin something.*

Whether or not Joseph's dreams sustained him during his betrayal, slavery, and imprisonment is impossible to know. If they did his life can serve as a powerful example of how sustaining expectations can be, regardless of how painful the journey. On the other hand, it is very difficult to imagine that Joseph did not – at least at some point – question his dreams. If he did question them, his life still serves as a powerful example of the fact that God – in spite of our own attitudes – never gives up on the dreams that He gives us. The issue, of course, is discerning between God's dreams for us and our ambition. Sometimes they look very similar.

Whether Joseph's dreams sustained him through his trials or if God protected and kept those dreams alive for him, his life is a powerful portrait of endurance. By virtue of Joseph's "sentness" and his trials and accomplishments in Egypt, Joseph is an excellent model of a leader who was sent.

Joseph was sent by God to save lives, bring deliverance and order to a world in crisis, and preserve a remnant. What a significant responsibility and role. Joseph's life gives us some of the essential pieces of what a sent leader does. According to Joseph's own testimony he was sent for the express purpose of:

1. Preserving life

2. Preserving posterity
3. Saving lives

To preserve life

Joseph first declared he was sent to preserve life. Quite literally Joseph was saying God sent me here to revive you. Joseph was not implying revival in terms of an old-school tent meeting. He wasn't sent there to be an evangelist. Rather he was sent to replace death with life, he was sent there to solve a problem, a very real and serious problem. Pharaoh and the Egyptians didn't care that he was a Hebrew or that he served a non-Egyptian God the only thing they were concerned about was if he could make a difference.

An important insight from this is that sent leaders sometimes make a difference without others even knowing that they are Christians. This is not something that should be condemned; it is not as if they are ashamed of the gospel, quite the contrary. The fact is simply this; when a problem is volatile enough few people care about the faith of the problem solver – they only care that the problem gets solved.

Sometimes the room your gift makes for you is dangerous. It may land you in circumstances of high consequence, which can be scary, ambiguous, or chaotic.

When Joseph arrived in the palace of Egypt death was imminent. The death and destruction of famine were going to be a reality, God had already revealed it. Joseph's arrival in the palace was probably not the glorious realization that we imagine. Joseph was there because all of Egypt, including Pharaoh, was scared about the uncertain future and they didn't know what to do about it. It was a highly stressful, highly volatile situation, not a coronation.

Joseph found himself in staring ambiguity in the face. It is quite possible after he realized the size of the bite he just bit off, that he was nervous about being able to swallow it.

I often wonder at what point in the conversation with Pharaoh he realized where his gift of dream interpretation was taking him and the size of the problem he was going to have to solve as a consequence of it. Proverbs 18:16 says, "Your gift makes room for you." That is certainly an understatement in Joseph's case. Sometimes the room your gift opens to you is in a dangerous place. It may land you in circumstances of high consequence, which can be scary, ambiguous, or chaotic. It is important not to mistake that scary place for being in the wrong place.

Regardless of Joseph's frame-of-mind, it is likely that he didn't see his promotion from prison to the palace as a fulfillment of his destiny, but he was ready non-the-less.

Over the past 20 years of observing ministry, I have come to realize that apostolically-minded leaders don't always realize what they just volunteered for. But, I have also come to know that once they realize it they don't regret it. Apostolically-minded leaders believe that God will give them the grace to survive what God sent them to do. Whenever it was that Joseph realized his promotion and fame were about to land him in an incredibly difficult situation his faith took over.

A situation where God has the opportunity to show off is one of the most intense desires of a leader who is sent. For some reason, they just love it when the problem at hand can't be solved with man-made solutions. Supernatural insight is what is needed in these situations. David said, "I have more understanding than my teachers (Ps. 119:99)," he was not being arrogant, but he was speaking of the supernatural insight he had as a result of his knowledge of God. Joseph also experienced this and used his supernatural insight to give life.

One of the things that sent leaders must be able to recognize is death, and once recognized, displace it with life. This requires faith or what others might call extreme measures; measures that not all leaders are willing or capable of taking. Joseph was sent into a situation that was not merely chaotic, but where death was imminent.

Let me illustrate the difference. A gardener's responsibility is to plant flowers and grow life. Regardless of where the planting takes place cultivating and sustaining life is hard work. All leaders must do this. But depending on the type of land the gardener has available that job can be dramatically different. Imagine a gardener is sent to a plot of land where the soil is rich; the ground is tilled, and ready to be planted. In this case, the gardener plants the seeds, waters and protects his seeds, and waits for the signs of life. Now consider that the same gardener has been sent to a junkyard, a landfill, full of garbage, trash, and hard cracked dirt, and is asked to plant in toxic soil. This type of situation is a different job entirely. The amount of work that must go into the preparation of the soil may be unprecedented. The soil must be detoxified, the ground must be broken up and tilled, rocks, debris, and trash must be removed. Joseph wasn't just asked to preserve life he was asked to preserve and sustain life in a toxic landfill. This is the unique assignment of many apostolic leaders. Most apostolic leaders are not sent into a church or ministry with a thriving membership, healthy people, an awesome facility, no debt and a huge budget. The reality is often the junkyard scenario.

There is something about the sent leader that relishes the opportunity to not only plant seeds and bring forth life but to plant those seeds in hostile and unforgiving places. Joseph did and did it well. His entire life he was surrounded by hostile and toxic soil. His brothers hated him, his work environment was drowning in the spirit of seduction, he was falsely accused of committing the sins that were actually perpetrated against him, he helped people and they forgot about him, the list goes on. Joseph got a raw deal and it's hard to argue otherwise. But all of these raw deals – to which he probably did not see an end – God used for good and ended up being a critical training ground for his ultimate challenge of saving the world.

Perhaps it is this sentiment that Paul is trying to convey when he describes how undesirable it is to be an apostle (1 Corinthians 4:13). I think it is safe to come to the conclusion that having an apostolic assignment is not nearly as glamorous or rewarding as many modern day depictions of the apostolic are said to be. If you're favored enough to receive an apostolic assignment chances are you will be needed in a junkyard far more often than a greenhouse.

For posterity

The second reason Joseph said he was sent was so that he could preserve a posterity for his brothers. Posterity is an interesting word, it is a noun referring to all future generations. Sent leaders understand and deal with the future differently than most other leaders. Foresight, not hindsight, is a major motivator.

Preserving a posterity meant that Joseph was sent ahead to ensure that there would be a remnant of people who knew what God had done. This also means he was sent to ensure there would be a legacy for his father. This fact is extremely significant! Joseph's brothers were not exactly the most honorable men. They very well might have stayed home and let their families die of starvation – thinking and believing there was nothing they could do. If they had done this their shortsightedness – or inability to properly relate to the future – would have ended an entire race of people. Joseph was sent away from the toxic environment of his brothers into the toxic environment of Egypt, but at least, in this new place, he would learn how to relate to the future properly.

I believe a sent leader's authority is delegated to them so that the proper honor and legacy is set up for those who preceded him or her. Sent leaders have the unique ability to articulate what they see in the future as a present-day reality while at the same time being able to honor and recognize the contribution and value of the past.

I believe that it is a distinguishing characteristic of apostolically-minded leadership to defer honor for anything that is accomplished to a preceding generation. Additionally, apostolically-minded leaders are aware of how their actions and the actions of those around them impact the future. One of the roles that Joseph was sent to fulfill was to ensure that history remembered accurately the God of Abraham, Isaac, and Jacob. Joseph could not have known what God had in store for the Israelites as slaves in Egypt, but Joseph's presence was preemptive on the part of God to prepare them for the future.

Saving lives

Finally, Joseph declared he was sent to save lives. This is obviously related to his calling to preserve life. However, there are some subtle differences. Saving lives implies that Joseph was given authority so that he could use his influence, resources, insight, revelation, and understanding to solve problems that would have otherwise ended in the death of thousands or even millions of people. This can serve as an illustration of the burden that is felt by those who are sent by God to lead. Sent leaders have a heavy burden to carry. Sent leaders take seriously their responsibility and understand the heavy burden that comes with their assignment. Ultimately they understand that people's lives are in the balance. This reality adds a sense of urgency and importance to their work and is why they often stand out in a crowd.

Joseph's journey

Joseph was uprooted from his home, land and family; he was torn from all that was familiar to him and sent to foreign soil. Apostolically-minded leaders may find that their authority is only good in certain places. It is tempting to believe that authority and gifting are needed and appreciated everywhere, but that is not always the case. Delegated authority is given for specific spheres and has implications for people and places one may not even be aware of. Sometimes it is easy to find the sphere God has intended and sometimes it is not. When it is not, regardless of the authority and destiny you may have, it is of the utmost importance to maintain the heart of the servant until that sphere is made clear.

Joseph endured many things that all of us would consider unfair; he was hated, sold into slavery, falsely accused, and forgotten in prison. All these different circumstances were tests of Joseph's staying power and faith. Joseph's calling and his ability to accurately hear God's voice were not on trial. Joseph knew God gave him his dreams, and may have even been fairly sure he knew the implications of his dreams, but what Joseph did not know was the timing.

The issue needing settled in Joseph's heart was would he hold onto what God had said, regardless of the circumstances? The same question applies to all leaders today, regardless of your sphere or level of authority; will you hold onto God's word and His dream for you even in the face of insurmountable odds and uncertainty? Successful leaders usually do and sent leaders must.

The glory of the call and the potential to excel as a leader is an awesome thing and can help build momentum for ministry; but how does a leader create momentum when there is none, even when it appears as if God has taken away any momentum? Joseph's life shows how.

From obscurity to authority

Marks of an apostolic leader are many and vary from person to person and situation to situation, but one thing is certain, just as in the case of Joseph, an apostolic leader is sent to a place or to intervene in a circumstance in a time of crisis, to bring balance, order, and lessen the degree of difficulty that potentially might happen. Joseph's journey began in hatred, jealousy, and led to slavery and imprisonment, but ended in victory.

Joseph's true test of leadership did not occur until seven years into his governing.

God sent Joseph to Egypt, and although his first seven years as a leader in Egypt may have been pleasant, the next seven proved to be the true testing of his leadership and authority. It was during the famine – the second seven years – when his leadership ability was truly challenged, not before! Yes, Joseph passed several tests on his way to Egypt's helm, but those tests where tests of the heart, tests that proved him a true servant. Notice Joseph had zero leadership credentials when he took the helm in Egypt. In fact, as far as Pharaoh knew he was a condemned rapist. We have no reason to believe – the Bible does not give any indication – that his name was ever cleared. All of Joseph's tests along the way were between Joseph and God, about his heart and attitude, not even his brothers or father knew what or how he was doing.

When Joseph finally came to Egypt, Pharaoh had no inclination nor did he likely care about Joseph's previous life, his failures, his frustrations, his proven character, or servant's heart. He just needed someone to save Egypt from impending disaster. Did Joseph have gifts? Yes. Would those gifts have been enough without testing? No. Pharaoh may not have considered Joseph's journey, but God did! A servant's heart may not have been important to Pharaoh, but it was (and still is) important to God.

For those sent leaders assigned and equipped to lead in the marketplace, be aware that the people in that marketplace may not care if you have been tested as a servant. This fact makes the marketplace dangerous. The marketplace is likely to be more concerned with your gifting. It is likely they need you for your gift, which is yours to use, whether you are tested or not. However, having a gift does not mean you have received the necessary authority to use that gift to its full and intended purpose. It is important to remember there is no shortcut in God's development process. If you yield too early to the allure of position and rank in the marketplace without having been properly tested it can lead to ruin. Imagine what might have happened to Joseph if Egypt had suffered any significant loss from the famine. He might have been returned to prison, beaten, revealed as a fraud, maybe even killed. Worst of all he would have forfeited reconciliation with his brothers, surrendered the legacy of his father's family, and contributed to the collapse of a nation. All under the pretense of being something he was not. There are personal and community consequences to acting impatiently or assuming authority too quickly. You should always accept any promotion with caution and reverence.

Joseph's true test of leadership did not occur until seven years into his rule. Many people consider Joseph to have reached his destiny the day Pharaoh called him out of prison, changed his name, put a robe on his back and a ring on his finger. I do not believe that. His true destiny came seven years after the ring was put on his finger and disaster struck the land. It was then when it was proven if the years in slavery, imprisonment, and being hated by those who should have loved him made him the man he needed to be to save the world.

The day Pharaoh called him out of the dungeon was not the realization of his destiny. It was a personal validation between him and God. God conferred His authority on a man, in the form of an assignment, which enabled him to use his gifting in the palace of a pagan king. The fulfillment of his destiny and dream came much later, well over seven years later. If nothing else, Joseph's life is a model of leadership endurance and waiting.

Different spheres of authority

In the journey from obscurity, Joseph graduated through several levels or spheres of authority. A sent leaders influence and authority has boarders and boundaries. Authority is never unrestrained or all inclusive. The authority of an apostolic leader is marked by spheres.[2] Joseph experienced these spheres as well; he started with favor in his father's house, which is a symbol of the local church. No apostolic leader is without an origin or place of beginning. Joseph was first a blessing to his father and found favor there. Sent leaders must start as laborers in their Father's house, it's there where gifting, callings and destiny take shape and are developed.

Next we find Joseph as a blessing to Potiphar; note that his sphere has increased. Because of his faithfulness and discipline, which he learned in his father's house, he was able to excel at the next level. He was given charge over every one of Potiphar's belongings and servants and proved to be faithful there. He later found himself having favor in the eyes of his jailer, and was given charge over the Pharaoh's prisoners; this was a much larger responsibility with much heavier consequences for failure. I cannot speculate what would have happened if a prisoner were to escape under Joseph's charge, but as a prisoner himself, it probably would have been pretty bleak for Joseph.

Finally, Joseph found himself before the Pharaoh, king of all Egypt, and ultimately second in authority. Despite his circumstances and obstacles Joseph was elevated from place to place, increasing in authority along every step. I believe he was given successively greater spheres of authority because he was first faithful in his father's house. Even though he wasn't always present with his father he always remained faithful to his father's house as was demonstrated by his declaration of feeling an obligation to preserve a posterity for his brothers. For us today, we can use this, as an illustration, to demonstrate that no matter how great a promotion is or how far it takes you from home you will still always be responsible for being faithful and accountable to the local church.

Joseph was able to excel, move in authority and bring peace into difficult circumstances because he did not try to exercise authority beyond his sphere. Taking Potiphar's wife not only would have been a sin against God, but he also would have overstepped his pre-defined sphere of authority. Because he stayed within his sphere in Potiphar's house by not taking what wasn't his, he was later able to increase his authority.

Joseph was able to learn these lessons in the process of living. It was in the middle of being hated by loved ones, made to be a slave, imprisoned, and falsely accused of a terrible crime when he was promoted. Leaders need to be able to see past the circumstances of life and understand that everything can be used to sharpen your skills for that day when the famine hits. The question is, who among us prepares for a famine when we have such a wounded past to deal with? To do this requires an ability to relate to the future by practicing foresight (more on that on page 96).

Spirit of excellence

It is clear, from the entire account of Joseph's life and experiences, that he was a man of excellence. True – he may have been a little arrogant, but everything he touched seamed to prosper. The Lord had given him a special grace to see things prosper. I call this the spirit of excellence. Excellence is something of outstanding or high quality. The Hebrew origin of excellence is the word *ga'ah* and means to mount up or rise.[3] Excellence carries the connotation of having the ability to rise above, rise above circumstances, rise above adversity, and to rise above accusations, which is exactly what Joseph did. No matter where he found himself he rose above the false accusations, temptations, and betrayals. In fact, he literally rose above all the other leaders to become a leader of leaders in a land not his own.

Another testimony of a sent leader is the ability to transcend the trappings and pressures of culture, society, ethnicity, and customs. When God delegates authority that authority comes with an optional use passport to bypass what holds others back. Apostolic leaders must exercise the ability to transcend culture, denominational bias, traditions and customs in order to be the leaders God intends. This is part of the spirit of excellence and is a divine endowment of a supernatural God. It is the sent leader who has this divine courage to stand in the face of trials and rise above each and every one to see peace established. The apostolic anointing breaks the yolk of disorder and brings clarity to chaos.

The spirit of excellence is marked by the ability to ascend into leadership even in an adverse situation. Every man and women should conduct themselves in excellence, but a spirit of excellence takes it one step further. Operating in an excellent spirit is more than just putting your best foot forward and giving it your best effort, it implies having the nature of excellence, a "Midas touch" as it were, where all things seem to be effected for the better just because you are there. Laban benefited from this same spirit of excellence when Jacob was dwelling with his family. The scriptures point out that as long and Jacob was around Laban was blessed.[5]

What a powerful lesson, both Jacob and Joseph were able to somehow learn the importance of promoting and serving another man's wealth and destiny before their own. The spirit of excellence was Joseph's inheritance. Note it is not demonstrated by mistake-free living. But, it is demonstrated when someone uses their talents, gifts, abilities, and authority to promote and serve another's vision and destiny.

Because of the spirit of excellence, everything Joseph put his hand to was blessed, and everyone around him was blessed. It does not mean that everything came easily, that is certainly not the case, but everything was fruitful. As modeled by Joseph, a sent leader has the ability to rise above and be prepared at any time to be called upon. In other words, you may never know when your gift will make room for you, so always be ready. The spirit of excellence gives you a "divine edge" in extinguishing the enemy's fiery darts. Despite all of Joseph's painful past, he was a blessing to his father, Potiphar, the jailer, Pharaoh, the nation, and ended up being a life-saving blessing to his bothers and his father's house.

Leadership lessons

We first hear of Joseph when he is seventeen years old and he was deliberately trying to get his brothers in trouble. Not as noble a beginning as one might think. He was mad that his brothers were not treating him well so he told his father. He was as most little brothers are, a tattletale.

At first glance, many young leaders with apostolic assignments may appear petty, as if they are arrogant. This was the case with Joseph. He was the youngest, the least experienced, and still was favored over the other children. His brothers hated him for it and their hatred grew as more favor was revealed. Furthermore, Joseph's brothers envied him and as is the case with envy others always seems to be accused of arrogance and pride.

It likely appeared that Joseph was arrogant, after all, it seems to be apparent that he liked to gloat. Remember when he was telling his dreams to his father, the one who understood and loved him the most, rebuked him, not because the dreams were false, but because he broke protocol with his brothers.[6] What was happening was that Joseph knew something they did not. Apostolic leaders are vanguards in that they usually know or perceive something before others see it. This is not always a blessing. This becomes a challenge to the leader, in that there may be no legitimate confirmation from others. This can also be a challenge to the followers because they are being asked to do something they cannot see. For some that may appear to be arrogant.

This key unlocks the fact that despite age or experience, God will still plant a seed in the heart of His leaders and leave that seed at the discretion of the recipient. Joseph was young, naïve, and inexperienced, but God told him anyway. Here we have a young man receiving insight and a grandiose call from God and the first thing he does is begin spouting off at the mouth about how great God is going to make him and how all his brothers will be subjugated to his authority. This display was then (and still is now) frowned upon, especially if who you are telling your teachers and elders, who have more experience, more wisdom, and more ability, that they are going to have to come under your authority. Not wise, no matter how many times God tells you.

The nature of a true dreamer is to serve the dreams of others – not be a slave to their own dream.

Notice, God did not tell Joseph of the impending trials that would come with that authority. What God held back from Joseph may have kept him from acting. Would Joseph have been as quick to speak, if God showed him all the years as a slave and prisoner? Always keep in mind that God may choose to hold back key information so that your excitement will build, which may keep you from quitting. Sometimes knowing that we win, in the end, is all there is to get us through to the end.

Perhaps the first lesson Joseph learned on his journey toward leadership was, "keep my mouth shut" and only reveal what God has shown me when he says it is time. Not everybody will be enthusiastic about what God has said or about your destiny. There will be some who, like his father, keep the matter in mind for later; but, by-in-large people will not understand or know where you are coming from and "tag" you as arrogant and self-promoting. These misrepresentations and hasty judgments may be the first obstacles apostolic leaders must get through. They can be avoided by learning to be patient and serving quietly. However, these perceptions also serve as the first of many valuable lessons on tact, grace, and timing, the earmarks of a seasoned leader.

The dreamer

Joseph was a dreamer. His life was marked by dreams, not just his own dreams, but the dreams of others. More important to his destiny than his own dreams were the dreams of others. After all, it was Pharaoh's dream that was the catalyst for his rise out of the dungeon. Joseph learned the most important lesson any leader worth their salt can learn. That lesson is to interpret the dreams of others. Joseph was an interpreter of dreams and it made him stand out in the crowd.

Many leaders have become slaves to their dreams and therefore are driven by a selfish ambition that is masquerading as prophetic destiny.

Joseph was not able to walk in the fulfillment of his dreams or destiny until he helped others realize their dreams. This too is an earmark of a great leader, no man or woman can ever fully fulfill their God-given destiny or lead others unless they first support, adopt, embrace, and help fulfill another person's dream. Helping others fulfill their dreams marks the spirit of a dreamer.

The nature of a true dreamer is to serve the dreams of others – not be a slave to their own dream. Many leaders have become slaves to their dreams and, therefore, are driven by a selfish ambition that is masquerading as prophetic destiny. Joseph started out as a slave to his own dream and consequently was not able to relate to others over anything but his own dream. Eventually he learned to be a servant to the dreams of others. Helping others realize their dreams became the turning point for Joseph and marked his ascension to greater authority and influence.

God can always work with someone who is willing to serve and promote the dreams of others. The only corporate ladder in God's economy involves promoting others by being the stepping rung to someone else's greatness.

Sent leaders who have a long tradition of difference making have done so because they have made a life of serving. The scripture is clear, that to be great, you must be a servant of all.[7] All leaders, no matter where you have come from or where you have ended up must promote people. No leader will be of any consequence unless the people know that they are there to serve, build, and protect.

Strong character

Imagine with me for a moment the temptation Joseph may have felt in Potiphar's house. The Bible does not say he was tempted, but it is not unrealistic to think he might have dealt with some temptation. Joseph was the master of Potiphar's house, he managed everything. In fact, the scripture declares that Potiphar so trusted Joseph that he did not even know what all he had.[8] Joseph easily could have gotten away with adultery or theft. He had command of every servant and slave. What is more, Potiphar's wife tried to seduce him every day.[9] This onslaught must have been an extremely difficult situation to manage emotionally and logistically. Joseph's innocence and purity won out in the end, although only he, Potiphar's wife, and God knew it. Regardless of what other people thought Joseph he was a pure and upright man. However, to withstand this daily temptation, knowing full well that it would be easy to get away with speaks volumes of the depth of Joseph's integrity and character.

Joseph experienced temptation; he was a young man and was not married. His faith, purity, and character prevented him from violating God and sinning against his body and his master. I do not believe it was Potiphar that Joseph was concerned about offending, I believe he knew he could have gotten away with it, but he did not want to sin against God. Character and purity are two pillars leaders must build to earn the kind of authority God desires to give. Joseph modeled for us the kind of unwavering purity necessary to be sent, and it made him stand out in a crowd.

Ironically, it was this same noble purity and character that led Joseph to prison. Suffice to say, people do not always understand or respond to Godly purity and character, in fact, they may even despise it. It is possible that they may even use it against you, say you are weak, or unable to make the hard decision.

Foresight

Having foresight is superior to having a dream. Foresight is the ability to see past the obstacles that are in front of your dreams. Dreams are common, everyone has one. But not everyone can see a path to their dream. Note that those who fail to achieve their dream, can still see it out there, they just can't see a way around the obstacle in front of them. They have, what I call the "I-can't-because-problem." They see their dream, but tell themselves, "I can't do it because... (you fill in the blank). For example, I want to write my novel, but I can't because I have no time or I want to finish my education, but I can't because I have no money. This behavior demonstrates an absence of foresight. Joseph never said that to himself. He served through his obstacles (and there were many). Serving is the proof that foresight is present! The way around the obstacles in front of your dreams is to serve. Serving obliterates the obstacles on your path.

Joseph's entire life was marked by service, dedication, and loyalty in spite of where he was or whom he was serving. He learned to place service at a premium. Perhaps the greatest insight we have of what Joseph learned in his journey is seen by what he did during the seven years of plenty as governor of Egypt. During the years of plenty, we have unique insight into his mind with the naming of his sons.

Joseph had two sons and he named his first Manasseh and his second Ephraim, which means fruitfulness. Manasseh literally means "I have forgotten" and he named his son that because he had "forgotten the toil in his father's house." What an awesome testimony. Before fruitfulness can happen there must be a forgetting or setting aside of the past. A painful and resolved past has a tremendous capacity to stifle destiny. Joseph truly was sent by God and not his brothers, what his brothers intended for evil, God meant for good.

9

Apostolic Assignment of Moses

Come now, therefore, and I will send you to Pharaoh that you may bring My people, the children of Israel, out of Egypt.
Exodus 3:10

    Leaders typically remain unnoticed until there is a crisis. It is then that a leader arrives to take a group to a new place. Successful leaders transition people from one place to another. This aspect of leadership is a type of deliverance. Deliverance is a critical task of those God sends. Perhaps this is why it has been said true leadership is demonstrated in times of crisis. It is in a crisis when a deliver is needed most. All of our apostolic prototypes, so far, have been delivers of sorts. Adam was sent to subdue the earth, which means take dominion over hostile forces. Joseph was sent to deliver Egypt and his family from certain death, and Moses was sent to deliver the nation of Israel out of their affliction and cruel bondage, and as we will see David and Nehemiah were also deliverers. Suffice to say sent leaders are aware of their responsibility to help people transition and sometimes that transition is dramatic and radical.

Moses is a great example of an Old Testament model of apostolic leadership, not only because he was sent to deliver, but because he demonstrated many aspects of delegated authority. Aspects that are relevant today. Moses' life is the epitome of this type of leadership; because he experienced divine favor, unique authority, had an awesome revelation of God, and received divine plans and blueprints as a builder. These and others aspects of his life are truly representative of his sentness and enabled him to stand out in a crowd.

Successful leaders transition people from one place to another.

Moses' story begins in troubled times, under difficult circumstances. Out of fear, Pharaoh ordered that all the male children of Hebrew women be drowned. The whole intention of Pharaoh's slaughter was to kill one person, Moses. Ironically, Moses was the only person he missed; and not only that, but Pharaoh ended up raising him in his own palace. Ironically, when you have favor with God not only does the enemy miss you when he tries to take you out but just for trying God forces that enemy to bless you; and your enemy is none the wiser for it!

From the very beginning, Moses had a special mandate. He was found by Pharaoh's daughter, nursed by his own mother, and raised in Egypt among the king's court as Pharaoh's grandson. Later Moses received his apostolic mandate directly from the Lord, during an encounter with the Lord at the burning bush. The Lord sent him to Egypt, to deliver the people and take them into their promised land (Exodus 3:10). Moses' adventure through

Pharaoh's court, to Midian, and back to Egypt can serve as a picture of several things, but first let's focus on the issue of divine favor.

Divine favor and grace

Moses lived, learned, and played in Pharaoh's court, eating the fat of the land, learning from the best teachers, and suffering little, while his kinsman suffered much. It appears to me that what often starts out as divine favor slowly becomes grace-to-endure (we have seen this in Joseph's case, and we will see in David's case too). Why does God allow seasons of favor, and then seem to exchange that favor with grace to endure only to give favor back again? I think it is because favor builds momentum. Without favor many of us would not venture out in the first place.

God allows these events to occur, but they are always for the refining and benefit of the leader and the followers. The transition from favor to grace builds a better leader, builds character, builds integrity and most importantly, it teaches the leader to trust God and to be sensitive to the direction of the Holy Spirit. Obviously, this dependence upon God is essential for all leaders, but is an absolute quality that must be embedded into the very fabric of all apostolic leaders. It is human nature to assume that success is in some way the result of human efforts, so invariably God must allow His leaders to go through times of failure. The favor that comes at the beginning serves to build momentum for what God has planned next. Without that favor, there is little momentum, the testing of the Lord may be hard, but the Lord nudges us by planting a sense of destiny in our hearts along the way.

Midian: Trained, untrained, & retrained

Pharaoh himself unwittingly spoils his own plan and saves out the very one that will later deliver the Israelites. God has a great sense of irony and often will grant leaders favor among their enemy, at least for a season. Later Moses sabotaged his favor by killing an Egyptian and is forced to become a fugitive in Midian. In Midian Moses experiences grace. I believe Moses killed the Egyptian because he did not understand the timing of God or his own destiny. Moses simply became impatient. It was not yet his time to save the slaves. He tried nonetheless in his own power to deliver the Hebrew slave and possibly ended up changing the trajectory of his life.

In Midian, Moses learned to be a faithful shepherd, came to understand his calling, was released, and ultimately sent, undoubtedly unlearning and relearning many of the necessary lessons he would need for his future endeavors.

Midian is a unique place. For Moses literally and us metaphorically it brings many essential issues to the forefront. Midian is a place all God's leaders must pass through. Midian is a dry desert place and means contention or quarreling.[1] It was no accident that this is the place Moses ended up after he tried to save an Israelite by his own strength. However, his strength only landed him in trouble, and his inability to see God's plan landed him in his "Midian experience."

It was in Midian where Moses argued and contended with God over the issue of the Israelites bondage and his own role and destiny. In killing the Egyptian, he acted out of God's timing and method. His motive of saving the Hebrew slave was noble, but self-motivated. As is often the case with great leaders, they arise from of a place of discontentment with the status quo. Like Joseph, it is not uncommon for a leader to know (or think they know) who they are before everyone else does. This awareness can sometimes lead the leader to act out of God's timing. Often that presumption leads to failure and raises questions of identity. I believe it was in Midian, Moses wrestled with God over his own identity and the meaning of Israel's bondage.

Midian is the place in the life of every leader, where one asks God, why? Midian is the place where you seem to quarrel with God, over issues that often end up being your life's passion. Moses went to Midian because he had issues with God, and God was not about to let Moses continue to do things his way without correcting his heart. In one way or another, all sent leaders experience their "Midian" and have to come to terms with their attitude, behavior, and purpose.

Sent leaders often see injustice and because of gifting are motivated to react. Reactionary leaders don't help much, so God allows Himself to be contended with, albeit only for a season, because God ultimately cannot be contended with (at least Moses escaped unscathed, Jacob was not so fortunate, (God gave him a permanent limp). However, the Lord allows these seasons in a leader's life so the realization of His design, His plan, and His purpose can be born in their heart.

It was exile that created Moses, the leader.

Moses eventually graduated from Midian, because he came to realize that it was no use arguing with God. God will always prevail so it is best to learn the lesson as quickly as you can. For Moses, that took 40 years. Moses' encounter with God at Midian resulted in his understanding of, and submission to God's superior plan. This lesson proved to be invaluable, as Moses led Israel through the desert.

Varied experiences

Moses' journey went from Pharaoh's grandson to prince, to murderer, to shepherd, to deliverer, to leader and prophet. I believe as a young man, Moses was eager to lead, his education in Egypt and the palace prepared him for a certain type of leadership that he wanted to demonstrate. But his training in Midian, as a shepherd, taught him that leadership is not glamorous. Midian is often a time of unlearning and relearning. Moses had to unlearn the secular form of leadership and relearn it God's way. And, I am convinced that this process happens in Midian.

Moses became a cautious leader maybe even reluctant. He wasn't always cautious. He learned to be. In fact, he outright did not want the job and when he finally did accept his role as leader he sometimes let his temper and frustration get the better of him. Consider this prayer of Moses, a genuine leader's prayer:

> *"So Moses said to the LORD, "Why have You afflicted Your servant? And why have I not found favor in Your sight, that You have laid the burden of all these people on me... I am not able to bear all these people alone, because the burden is too heavy for me."*[2]

Leadership is definitely a journey of ups and downs. There were times that the frustration of leadership seemed too great for him to handle, but there were other times when God wanted to kill the people and Moses stood before God on their behalf to save these same people. Consider the words of God to Moses:

> *"Now therefore, let Me alone, that My wrath may burn hot against them and I may consume them. And I will make of you a great nation." Then Moses pleaded with the LORD his God... So the LORD relented*

*from the harm which He said He would do to His people."*³

Moses experienced both the joy and pain of leadership. The unique role of the apostolically-minded leader is to assume both roles, the role of advocate for the people, and ruler over the people. These two different roles may seem difficult to marry together, but the successful leader must find a way.

A shepherd and stranger

A fugitive often has a lot of time on their hands to think, to reinvent themselves, and to do a lot of self-searching. It was during his exile that Moses began to understand who he was. Ironically, it was also the place where he began to build a family and create a life for himself. This is a testimony to the fact that Midian is not all pain and agony. It was during his time of exile that Moses grew to maturity. He became a defender of the flocks, husband, father, and a responsible shepherd.

"Exile created Moses, the leader."⁴ As a fugitive, Moses was a stranger; in fact, he named his first son, Gershom, which means stranger. Moses was alone and felt out of place. I believe God allowed him to feel nameless, a little bit of what it was like to be a servant and slave to someone else while in Midian. I believe this loneliness motivated him to leave his routine and deliberately "turn aside" and see the "great sight" God had for him in the burning bush.

It seems that God always delegates authority to men and women who have an established tradition of excellent service.

All sent leaders go through a season of exile, self-searching, and personal discovery, where they often feel alone and misunderstood. This is Midian and is very necessary for the unlearning and relearning process. The call of God is a serious one, and should not be taken lightly.

It was during Moses' exile that he took to the job of shepherding. It is noteworthy that many of the Old Testament leaders who had a great impact came from solitary places or from a place of serving. Moses learned by shepherding. Joseph learned by serving Potiphar and his jailer, Adam by tending the garden, David was a shepherd and served Saul, Samuel served Eli in the temple, Esther and Nehemiah both served a king, it seems that God always delegates authority to men and women who have an established tradition of excellent service. No person, from any walk of life, can be great unless they are first and always a servant! A leader must always be a servant; the moment one stops serving the authority to lead stops with it. Moses learned to serve and heed the voice of his father-in-law in the desert, as an undershepherd to Jethro. This proved valuable, for it was later that Moses returned to Jethro for advice on how to rule and judge the people effectively.

The fact that Moses shepherded another man's flock is also extremely noteworthy. This reinforces what we learned about Joseph and how it is critical to build and promote another man's wealth, prosperity, and destiny. Moses could not yet be trusted with his own flock. In fact, God required that he be able to prosper another man's flock before he was released to have his own. It is no different today! God requires that every leader give their life, energy, blood, sweat, and tears to someone else's vision before entering into his or her own. In order to embrace someone else's vision you must let go of your own. Only after you are able to release your vision and learn to have satisfaction in serving others are you ready to move forward.

Turning aside and the reluctant leader

Nothing mentioned in the Bible is irrelevant. Do not let the detail that Moses intentionally "turned aside" escape your attention. It was not until the Lord saw Moses, "turn aside" that He spoke to him from the bush. If Moses had not turned aside to see he may have missed everything.

It is necessary to realize that it was not the Lord calling from the midst of the bush that caught Moses' attention, it was the strange sight. It was only *after* he turned aside to look that God called out to him. It was as if the Lord was waiting for Moses to do something. Often the Lord will require an effort on the part of his leaders that appears to be, on the surface, chasing something strange or unusual. This was a strange and unusual spectacle. Moses wanted to know more about it. He could have continued with his duties and dismissed it as a desert mirage, but he stopped to see. He turned aside from his routine to investigate the strange phenomena – something that had he tried to explain to a friend may have resulted in that friend thinking he was crazy.

Moses broke out of his routine to investigate a strange phenomenon. Sometimes that can be a divine distraction to get you back on track, a track you may not have even realized you were off. You can go about the business of leading and managing and maybe see some success, but God has an experience waiting for you that will give clear direction, clear information, and may even spell out the future for you, but it comes when you are willing to be interrupted by God. Being willing to be interrupted by God makes the difference between moderate successes and fulfillment.

Ironically, once Moses discovered what he was being sent to do, he became somewhat reluctant. Moses had tried and failed before. Any leader worth their salt will experience a certain amount of fear and reluctance – sometimes those feelings never go away, but do not confuse that with a lack of confidence. God can always work with a man or woman who is humble and dependent upon Him. Leaders must come to the place where God becomes the only source. He is the bread of life and no leader can offer anything of value to any person unless God has first captured their heart.

Moses was reluctant, he made excuse after excuse and even asked God to send someone more qualified. But it didn't work, God wanted Moses. So, He made Moses into the leader He wanted him to be. Interestingly, even in the midst of leading, Moses still needed guidance and direction on how to lead. Even at 80+ years old, Moses needed the assistance of other capable leaders, such as Aaron and Jethro. Both of these men – and others – became valuable assets to Moses's leadership development.

Revelation that leads to authority

Moses was a true friend of God. He spoke with Him face-to-face. His communication and relationship with God were unparalleled; perhaps only eclipsed by the communication that Adam had with God before the fall. Regardless, I believe Moses had unique access to God. This, of course, had to be one of the key distinctions to his authority. Not because no one else ever did or ever could have the level of contact with God the way Moses did, but because Moses knew there was no substitute for God's input. This is perhaps best shown by Moses' insistence that unless God went with him, he wasn't taking the people anywhere. How many of us would actually not move, in other words, make no decisions or plans unless God initiated it? Suffice to say, that may be too risky for many of us today, and is perhaps why we are always in so much trouble. Moses was willing to take that risk. Moses was more aware than anyone else of his inadequacy and knew that the only way he would be successful was if God was the initiator of everything that he did.

There is a certain level of authority that can only come from this kind of revelation. We have all heard the proverbial statement, "knowledge is power," well that is partly true. The whole truth of that statement is knowledge *of God* is power; or stated another way, "to know God is to have authority." Many men strive after knowledge because the more one knows the more power one may have. Information unlocks doors, creates ideas, and sets people apart. That is true in the practice of leadership and that is where the famous axiom "leaders are readers" comes from. However, in the arena of the spirit, there is a different type of knowledge that leads to authority and it is called revelation.

Attaining book knowledge and experience can be a great asset and may be a noble endeavor, but make no mistake, there is no substitute for being led by the Holy Spirit.

Attaining book knowledge and experience can be a great asset and may be a noble endeavor, but make no mistake, there is no substitute for being led by the Holy Spirit or knowing the Word of God. Apostolically-minded leaders do not replace Holy Spirit interaction for theories, models, or principles that can be attained from books. The chief and primary focus must be given to pursuing God's plan and His purpose for where God has sent you. Theories, models, and principles are not entirely worthless they just can never be allowed to distract you from the true source of revelation.

The Bible says that Moses spoke with God face-to-face. That alone is awesome. Moses had encounters with God that few men experience and this fact contributed greatly to his authority and influence. People knew he was with God by the signs he performed and the countenance of his face. Moses' face was physically altered (in a good way), which represented to the people he had been with God; so much, in fact, they could plainly see it on his face. This made him a trustworthy and a worthy role model for other leaders to follow. In fact, his protégé tried to mimic that exact aspect. We are told that Joshua lingered in the tent of meeting, alone with God. No doubt to gain an experience and knowledge of God he saw practiced every day by his teacher and mentor.

It seemed the Lord always revealed to Moses what he was going to do next. The Lord told Moses in advance about the plagues, their wilderness journey, the Red Sea, he received divine blueprints for the Tabernacle and he saw the entire Promised Land with his eyes before Israel entered in. It seems that during Moses' life God gave him a first look at His plans. This level of revelation was the fuel that ignited Moses' authority. Furthermore, it was this revelation that ultimately legitimized and validated Moses' leadership. If leaders would spend more time pursuing a revelation of God directly from His face – instead of from books and conferences – they might wield more authority and influence.

Carnally-minded leaders may try to hold onto their authority, sent leaders give it away.

God does not want His leaders to be in the dark, He intends for them to know where they are going and what is coming next. There are times when He requires leaders to walk by faith and put more trust in Him, but by-in-large I believe He wants to make His leaders aware of the next turn. He is waiting to communicate the future to His leaders if they are willing to listen, and turn aside from their plans and agenda. Moving in divine revelation is a better predictor of the future and instills greater authority than experience ever could. When you lack revelation experience is all you have to rely on. However, if you have revelation experience becomes even more valuable and you end up with exponentially greater insight.

Distributing authority

Moses integrates the role of manager and leader well. This ability is something we did not mention about Joseph, but Joseph did it too. Nehemiah is also an excellent example of a leader who learned to manage well, but Moses is our exemplar. He was able to take an overwhelming task and make it manageable. Leaders who are good managers demonstrate that by distributing authority to the right people, people who get things done.

Sent leaders must be visionaries and forerunners, but they do not use those characteristics as excuses to be inattentive managers. Sent leaders find a way to integrate visionary leadership with the task of day-to-day management. One of those management tasks is to maximize efficiency, so that hard tasks are made easier by team effort. Therefore, organizing and empowering teams is clearly a distinguishing mark of good managers. With the help of Jethro, Moses found ways to delegate authority to faithful elders, without abdicating his responsibility. Carnally-minded leaders may try to hold onto their authority, sent leaders give it away. An apostolically-minded leader accomplishes extra work by disseminating authority.

One important distinction is that sent leaders understand that authority, and not only responsibility, should be distributed.

The most effective use of authority is when it accompanies responsibility. For every responsibility that is delegated the proper amount of authority is needed to go with it. Some people only delegate responsibility – that is an unfortunate mistake.

The most effective leaders know that any authority they have is God's and not their own and that it was not attained by human effort, knowledge, or wisdom. In fact, Jesus Himself made it clear that the authority He had was from His Father (John 14:10; 16:13). The sent leader distributes authority generously because they know they themselves have been recipients, and that their own efforts or grasping after authority only frustrates the purpose of God.

Unabated strength

"Moses was one hundred and twenty years old when he died. His eyes were not dim nor his natural vigor diminished."[6] There are few other more potent signs of God's favor than Moses' longevity. Wow, after shepherding 40 years in the remote mountainside of Midian then wondering around in a desert-like wilderness for 40 more years, that's 80 years of hard labor. To not have lost any strength or vision at 120 years old is nothing short of fantastic! It is not uncommon for leaders, after years of service, to lose their vision and focus, but not so with Moses. I believe that Moses not only kept his natural sight, but that he never lost his original vision of what God had in store for His people. Moses was able to maintain his strength because he always kept God's vision before his eyes and God's voice in his ears. Moses did not allow the complaining and poor attitude of the people to dissuade him from what he knew God showed him, and the Lord preserved him because of it. All of the time Moses spent having face-to-face conversations with God gave him supernatural longevity and vigor.

Sent leaders remember what they learned in Midian and are convinced of the fact that God cannot be contented with. Therefore, what God says, God does, no use experimenting with an alternate way. Leaders who know this operate in a much higher level of faith. It is this faith, which allows them to maintain focus and keep sight of what God has revealed.

What God has revealed will come to pass, and for leaders who truly grasp this, they do not lose their vision or strength during a difficult journey. God allowed Moses to see a great many things and because he saw God, his vision never left him. The Promised Land eluded him, because of his disobedience, but nonetheless, God allowed him the peace to know that his legacy would be continued and his vision would be fulfilled through Joshua.

The legacy

One final lesson from Moses' apostolic assignment is the importance of legacy. Sent leaders leave a legacy of faithful people to lead in their place after they are gone. Not all leaders truly understand this. A legacy cannot be left in a book or a building. A legacy is only expressed though the people they trained and developed. Moses left a legacy – or posterity for Israel – in Joshua.

Joshua finished what Moses started. Even though Moses could not enter the Promised Land, the people would. This was only possible because he had been faithful to instill the same sense of vision and purpose that the Lord instilled in him to another. Moses' purpose was to get the people out of slavery to the Promised Land. He did. The next stage was for his legacy (Joshua) to do. Moses did not literally take Israel into the Promised Land, but he saw it and was able to successfully pass on his vision to Joshua, who did. Sent leaders are diligent in identifying, equipping, and releasing others to continue what they started.

It is unfortunate that not every leader leaves a legacy. However, one of the marks of someone who stands out in a crowd is to leave a legacy and invest in the next generation. God's people entered their proper and promised destiny because of Moses' investment in the next generation.

10

Apostolic Assignment of David

> So David went out wherever Saul sent him, and behaved wisely. And Saul set him over the men of war, and he was accepted in the sight of all the people and also in the sight of Saul's servants. I Samuel 18:5

Perhaps no biblical character captivates and inspires the imagination like David. Of course, we all recognize David to be the perennial giant slayer. Even those people who have never attended Sunday school know the David and Goliath story. But for those of us who did attend Sunday school we know that David was more than a giant slayer. He was a respectful and faithful servant, an inspiring and capable mentor, a passionate and devoted lover, a dedicated and loyal friend, a gifted and talented musician, worshiper, and songwriter, and a valiant and fearsome warrior. David's life is a rousing example of a leader with an apostolic assignment to establish the kingdom of God. David stood out from the crowd for a great many reasons, but it was his love for the house of God made him a man after God's own heart. Perhaps no one is scripture had a passion for the building a house for God more than David.

Work is not something that happens after you receive your assignment, work is something that must happen before you are eligible to receive an assignment.

I believe it was David's heart to establish a house for God that distinguished him from the crowd. David did not merely want to go to church or be a part of a church, but he wanted to design it and build it. David wanted to bring structure and order to God's house. This is perhaps the most convincing argument for his apostolic assignment. Likewise, today's leaders who have an apostolic assignment must also have a passion for building God's house.

Commissioned to work

Few things are more disheartening to a young boy than the command, "get to work!" The simple truth is that if you believe you are called to lead you cannot get away from the fact that God requires work. Work is a prerequisite for leadership. Work is not something that happens after you receive your assignment, work is something that must happen before you are eligible for an assignment!

Many of the leaders who were sent by God were called from the place of working.

- Joseph was working for his jailer when his promotion came,

- Moses was shepherding Jethro's flock when his promotion came,
- Nehemiah was serving in the King's court when his promotion came,
- Gideon was threshing wheat when his promotion came,
- Daniel was serving as one of the king's eunuch's before his promotion came,
- Samuel was serving Eli in the temple when his promotion came,
- Several of the disciples were called from their fishing boats when their promotions came,
- David was called from shepherding his father's flocks when his promotion came.

It seems that God has an inclination to send people who are busy doing something. It is interesting to me that some of the most iconic leaders in biblical history were not sitting around and waiting for an assignment from God. They were not in prayer lines asking for discernment and direction over their future or waiting in long lines at conferences hoping for prophetic words about their assignment. They were faithful, diligent, loyal, and dedicated workers in someone else's field when God called them.

There is a very obvious theme in God's leadership development process and that theme is working men and women get chosen to be sent. As we will see later, Nehemiah's capacity to do record-breaking building was that the people "had a mind to work." No doubt a reflection of his own work ethic. Likewise, David was called by God in the middle of another job, which is something that made him stand out in the crowd.

Giant killer, musician, lover, warrior are a few of descriptions that come to mind when describing David. However, before he was any of those things, he was a shepherd. David has many characteristics that qualify him as an apostolic leader, but one of the key aspects of his success rests on the fact he knew how to serve and understood his place. Sent leaders make a real difference in their organizations and the lives of the people they know because they understand how to serve and defer to others.

David's apostolic assignment

In 1 Samuel 18:5 we read that David was "sent" by Saul. As we have witnessed with the other Old Testament apostolic prototypes, a specific purpose is always tied to the initial sending. With David, we see that he was sent as a warrior to subdue and defeat the enemies of Israel. David established his reputation as a leader by proving his loyalty to his nation and King Saul and by putting his life in jeopardy for Israel. He too, like every other truly apostolic leader embraced and promoted another man's destiny and aspirations. What is interesting about David is that he knew he was to be the next king and still willingly submitted himself as a loyal servant to the unqualified man he was to replace.

When we first read of David being sent it is important to note what preceded that event. Ironically, it was Jonathan, the legal heir to Saul's throne, who believed in David's calling. In verse 4 of II Samuel 18 we read that Jonathan bestows to David symbols of authority and protection. He ceremonially gave David his robe, his symbol of authority as a prince of Israel, which was followed by his belt, sword, and bow and arrows. These gifts were symbols of strength and protection and a gesture by Jonathan that demonstrated he recognized God's assignment on David. By giving these gifts to David, he was making known his willingness to let David be the protector and deliver of Israel.

We know that Jonathan himself was a very capable warrior and would have been a good protector. We read of his exploits in 1 Samuel 13 when he and his armor bearer defeated an entire garrison of Philistines. I do not think that too many biblical scholars would argue that Jonathan deserved to be and would have been a much better king than his father. But Jonathan, the rightful successor, behaved in the most noble and honorable way by stepping aside and recognizing that it was someone else who had been sent.

Obviously, it was God that sent David, but if you take a moment and allow yourself to consider it from a natural perspective it was Jonathan who confirmed his sentness. It was Jonathan who gave his position to David. It was Jonathan's future authority, which he freely gave to David and that is why David never took authority from Saul when he had the chance. David understood delegated authority and he refused to take any authority that was not given to him. David knew his rule would come through Jonathan's authority as future king, so he did not preempt God's timing by assuming his rule before Saul's authority was gone. David did not know if at some point Saul was going to give it to him or if God was going to remove Saul, either way, David purposed in his heart not to take another's authority.

Saul was unwittingly compelled to send David because of the spiritual dynamic Jonathan put in place that day; and whether Saul was ignorant of it or not he had to follow God's plan, so he sent David as a warrior. Being sent authorized David to function in an assignment as a warrior and we read that David quickly became one of the greatest warriors (if not the greatest) that ever lived. I believe David prospered because he restricted himself to function within his sphere of authority and did not worry about other spheres he was not yet authorized to occupy.

When David was a warrior, he made more warriors. When David was a king, he made kings. Another lesson of delegated authority is that those operating in their God-given place of authority reproduce what they are assigned to be. Like produces like – or as God stated it in Genesis 1:11-12 – "the seed is in itself." Meaning the essence of what makes you what you are is what you will produce. When you are leading in your correct sphere with delegated authority from God you will find the principles of reproduction in operation, and it will be a natural outflow of who you are.

A warrior's heart

David was a warrior. He defeated his enemies. Any leader must be on the cutting edge of advancement. No sent leader is valid unless there is forward movement. This forward momentum is part of all apostolic assignments. David was a man of war, he was a champion. He defeated the Philistine champion, Goliath, to become a champion himself. Sent leaders are by nature champions; they overcome personal and corporate giants in their lives, organizations, and ministry to advance the people they are serving. This is an important key because personal advancement is not the goal of great leaders, climbing the corporate ladder is not what brings success. A sent leader is only successful when the people following them become as great at killing giants as they were. David made giant killers (II Samuel 21:19)!

What is equally as inspiring is how he behaved under pressure. After he was sent by Saul, David "behaved wisely." David did not allow the glory, the authority, or the leadership to go to his head. He behaved wisely, the soldiers knew it, the people knew it, and Saul knew it. David was a cut above the rest, he too, like Joseph and Daniel, had an excellent spirit. He came out of the fields, out of his father's house as the youngest, smallest and least qualified to lead; and he handled the authority of a king masterfully and wisely, even before he was crowned king.

The antithesis of David's leadership was Saul's leadership. Saul was only worried about himself. Saul had the potential to be a great king, but he left too many personal issues unattended. We read about Saul's commissioning in 1 Samuel 9. I have always thought it was interesting that the job Saul was sent to do before his commissioning resulted in failure. As we have already outlined David, Moses, Nehemiah, and Joseph all were competent workers before they were sent. Saul also had the chance to prove his competency as a servant and worker before his ordination, but he failed – he never did bring home those donkeys he was sent to find (1 Samuel 9:4). Saul was put in a position of leadership before he demonstrated that he was a competent and faithful worker! This would be the first of many failures in Saul's leadership.

One of the most obvious personal issues that hindered Saul was his personal concern with prestige and reputation. Many modern-day leaders deal with this same hindrance. The temptation to succumb to the trappings of fame and prestige are not in- and-of-themselves wrong. Every leader will face this, but it is wrong to succumb to it.

One never truly knows what they are made of until they have to work to promote someone else's ideas.

There are leaders today who have great potential and great skill, but will never be anything more than someone with potential because they are a type of Saul, only concerned about preserving their job and promoting their dream. The question every leader must ask is whose dream will I promote? The answer to that question will ultimately determine their level of authority and influence.

A model shepherd

David's capacity to behave wisely was probably because of his experience as a shepherd. Not many people can say they "behaved wisely" when given a promotion or became famous. This is unfortunate because no such promotion should ever be given until one would be expected to "behave wisely." Unfortunately, because of great gifting or talent, many people are promoted before they are given a chance to demonstrate their ability through serving – which is what happened to Saul. It should have been no surprise that David would have behaved wisely, but for some reason, it greatly angered Saul. Probably, because Saul had secretly hoped that with David's new-found power and popularity he would become corrupt, greedy, and power hungry. David's integrity ran too deep.

Like many before him, David too learned to handle his great calling by serving. Consider this, while his father and brothers were eating and celebrating with the prophet Samuel, David was an afterthought, left out in the fields to take care of their responsibilities. His father and brothers took him for granted, the servant boy, conceived in sin, an outcast; but it was in his place of service and brokenness where God spoke to him, where he learned to be a worshiper, where he learned to listen to God, where he learned to rely on God, and where he ultimately learned to lead. The lessons he learned as a shepherd of someone else's sheep would be the lessons he would verbally recall to mind when he was facing his own destiny in front of his giants.

When David was called out from the fields he never stopped serving and he never stopped shepherding. Because of his shepherding skill, God chose him and called him to shepherd all of Israel. Just as he killed the lion and the bear, to defend his father's sheep, he killed the enemies of Israel to defend God's people.

In God's economy greatness is always preceded by service. The tasks that seem like menial service build the man and build the leader. One never truly knows what they are made of until they have to work to promote someone else's ideas.

David learned to be patient by serving. That is why, even after he was anointed as king, and even after God tore the kingdom from Saul, David was willing to wait for his right time. Even though David knew he would have been within his right to take Saul's life when he had the chance, he refused and waited until God removed Saul. For David to remove Saul would have been premature and presumptuous. Waiting for God to promote and advance you is the only way to receive legitimate delegated authority! David knew this and is perhaps why Absalom's betrayal hurt so deeply. David proved to be willing to wait for God's timing, something – I believe – he learned while waiting patiently on the Lord in the fields with the sheep.

Giant killer

Apostolically-minded leaders find ways to overcome, and in their overcoming, they know that they must be completely dependent upon God. I heard a definition of leadership once that said, leadership is dependence upon God. This is definitely true. It is God who raises up and tears down, and all authority is appointed by God. That being true, there is no leader worth their salt who has any notion that anything they have accomplished could have been done without God.

Those who are sent know that their success is only because of God's grace. David made this clear when he declared that it was God who would give him the victory over Goliath.

Goliath means "to expose or disgrace" and by implication to bring shame.[2] Goliath shamed and disgraced his opponents by exposing their weaknesses and their faults in front of others; he was an accuser and blame-bringer. Goliath was a symbol of Satan, the accuser of the brethren. On the other hand, David is a type of Christ. David's choice of weapons proved his greatest asset against his enemy. David's weapon was a stone. A stone cannot be created by human hands. David chose a weapon that he could not have manufactured. It was not a carnal weapon, but a weapon mighty through God, and with that weapon he was able to pull down his enemy (c.f. II Corinthians 10:4).

In the valley, that day against Goliath David faced accusation and shame and overcame it, not by his own effort, but with a supernatural weapon carved by the hand of God. This can teach us that one of the indications that a person is ready to enter into their place of delegated authority is when they have faced and overcome the secrets of their life that bring them shame and embarrassment.

David was outraged, not only at the Philistine's words but also by the fact neither Saul nor his army would face this giant. David experienced a bit of righteous indignation. He adopted another's cause and arose to fight this Philistine.

Whose battle was this anyway? Another mark of David's unique leadership was the fact he adopted someone else's battle. This was Saul's battle. However, because Saul was unwilling to defend God and Israel David took the place that should have been Saul's. He did what Saul was supposed to do.

David came out of the place of adversity and chaos to lead against the enemy of God's people. Leaders usually arise when there is great need. This was certainly one of those times. Israel needed a champion. The current leader was not willing to accept the risk to advance God's people. David rose to fight this Philistine and to save face for Saul, Israel, and God. David fought because he was concerned about God's reputation. All sent leaders should be motivated by preserving, protecting, and promoting God's reputation. No matter what setting the leader is sent to (the church or the marketplace) God's reputation is worth fighting for. By rising to fight in a time of crisis, David made a statement to the Philistines, to Israel, to Saul, and to God that he was capable of assuming the responsibility.

Let me briefly address Saul's dilemma with Goliath. Here was Goliath hurling accusations and profanity at Israel's God and king. I Samuel 17:11 states, that upon hearing Goliath's words, Saul and the Israelites were terrified. Saul was a cowered and spawned other cowards. The primary indicator of Saul's weakening leadership is that no one would fight Goliath for Saul. What is worse no one would defend their God. Author and retired Army officer, Richard Phillips states that, "The biggest indicator of Saul's failing leadership was the unwillingness of any of his followers to answer the challenge."[3] If true leaders produce other leaders, then it also must be true that cowards produce cowards. He was a failure and until David arrived to defend his God and king, there was no true leader in Israel.

David's legacy

Another signpost of David's sentness was that he reproduced other giant killers. We have already made several statements supporting the fact that leaders reproduce leaders. David certainly met this requirement. I Chronicles 11-12 briefly outlines the stories of David's mighty men. Of David's mighty men, there were those who defeated giants, Goliath's brothers, one even killed a lion on a snowy day in a pit.

Benaiah so much wanted to be like David that he jumped into a pit to kill a lion – oh, and by-the-way it was snowing. I have never tried it, but I am told the most dangerous lions are the ones backed into a corner. This didn't matter to Benaiah he saw an opportunity to kill a lion – like his mentor had – and he wasn't going to let the opportunity pass. No doubt that during their time together in the Cave of Adullam he recalled hearing David's stories of how he killed lions to save his father's sheep.

Another story tells that David was thirsty and three of his men risked their lives, broke through enemy lines, to get David water from Bethlehem. These men were willing to put their lives on the line for their leader. What a stark contrast to Saul, who could not motivate even one of his soldiers to engage Goliath for him or his kingdom.

Another one of David's mighty men fought so many and for so long that his hand stuck so that he could not let go of his sword. Biblical scholars believe it "stuck" because of the volume of blood spilled was so great that it completely covered and scabbed over his hands essentially bonding his hand to the hilt of the sword. But what valiance, what heroism, what courage! David reproduced in his men the same fighting spirit that he operated in and in doing so reproduced some of the mightiest men the world has ever seen.

David was a master at leaving a legacy. He not only reproduced in his warriors his own DNA, but he also left an ambitious and worthwhile responsibility for his son. Solomon's life was another legacy of David's. David left for Solomon a posterity. What greater compliment is there to a man than having his son carry out his dreams? Solomon built the Temple that David had envisioned in his heart to build. Solomon ruled Israel in peace and to this day, there has never been a wiser man known in all the earth.

In reference to the planning and building of the Temple, David and Solomon (like Moses and Aaron – the strategist and his mouthpiece) are pictures of an apostolic and prophetic team. David represents the apostolic, he had the vision and was the architect; Solomon was the voice, or stated another way, the action behind the plan. The Temple could not have been completed, nor would God have had a habitation, if the prophetic and apostolic had not labored together. Like Moses, Aaron, David, and Solomon apostolic leaders today must have reliable co-laborers. In other words, a team is an absolutely essential weapon in the sent leader's arsenal. And, the best teammate for an apostolically-minded leader is a prophetically-minded companion.

It is interesting to note that at one time Saul was on the right track. There was a time when the people sang that Saul had killed his thousands. This certainly speaks to his ability as a warrior and protector, but all that Saul was able to hear in those songs was the second stanza, that David killed his ten thousands. The tragedy of this is that if Saul had understood leadership he would've recognized this as a major complement. After all, at this point, David was following in Saul's footsteps. I find it hard to believe that David was jealous of Benaiah when he told him the story of how he killed a lion in a pit on a snowy day. David could have perceived this as Benaiah trying to one-up him, but he didn't. I'm sure David congratulated him for a job well done! But Saul did not recognize David's success as a positive reflection on his own leadership; he perceived it as a threat. Saul allowed jealously into the relationship, which almost immediately began the downward spiral of disqualifying him for greatness as a leader. By refusing to see David as part of his legacy Saul disqualified himself as a great leader.

Triumph and tragedy of leadership

David had two predecessors that helped his leadership stand out. David's story is not complete without looking at these two figures. One, we have already begun to discuss, Saul. The other was Samuel. Both of them were leaders. One was a poor example and the other was a good example. Saul represented the best of what man has to offer relative to leadership, style, looks, charisma, and all the natural attributes that men look for in a leader. Although Saul had the natural look of success, he did not have the character. It just proves that natural talent and ability are no substitutes for character and integrity. There is a natural look to leadership that usually impresses onlookers, but not God.

Samuel was David's other predecessor. Samuel was an apostolic figure in his own right (and we will discuss it in chapter 11). David did well to have Samuel in his life! Samuel represented transition. He was the leader that transitioned Israel from the governing of the judges to a monarchy. He also helped transition a nation from one king to another. He was a change master!

Samuel mentored David and may have taught David to respect the voice of the Lord and accept correction. Something I suspect the prophet Nathan was thankful for. Samuel modeled good leadership for David, although Saul did not heed Samuel's knowledge and experience David did. It was Samuel who warned the Israelites of the treachery having a king would bring upon them (I Samuel 8:11-18). Samuel had a very difficult job of facilitating a transition between kingdoms. We know David's rule was successful and Saul's a failure. A portion of the credit for David's success belongs to Samuel. Without Godly mentors the probability of failure is dramatically increased.

There are two very valuable lessons that we get from observing how differently Saul and Samuel mentored David. The first is that a sent leader must always be able to take the good with the bad. Samuel represented the good and Saul the bad. It was no use for David to complain about Saul. God had a purpose for Saul in the life of David! For David to complain about the leader that he was being asked to serve under would have disqualified him and impugned his character. David understood that Saul had a purpose in his life, regardless of the challenges he presented. David would need to embrace what these challenges would teach him.

The second lesson is that every leader needs a Godly mentor. Fortunately, Saul wasn't the only model David had to follow. Sent leaders are always looking for men and women who have favor and influence with God to speak into their lives, even after they have ascended to a certain level of authority themselves. No leader regardless of how gifted, talented, anointed, or influential they are ever outgrow the need for a Godly mentor.

The self-encourager

Another hallmark of a sent leader is the ability to encourage themselves when there is no one around to be encouraging. Everyone needs encouragement from other people, but there will be times when everything appears to be ending and those around you will not be able to encourage you because they themselves are suffering. It is at those times the deepest darkest times, when sent leaders need to draw away and find the encouragement they need from within their own soul. David demonstrated the capacity to encourage himself. I Samuel 30 records a time when David and his men were returning home from battle; he and his men were emotionally and physically exhausted. They approached their homes and saw everything destroyed and their families gone. They could not handle it, they cried until they literally had no strength in their bodies. Upon seeing this devastation and loss, David's own friends decided that the best thing to do would be to kill him. In their fatigue and delirium they lost sight of their leader and sought to kill the very one who was their champion, the very one whom they sang songs about.

The sent leader must have a sense of calling and destiny that can outlive other's frustration and anger.

Two lessons can be learned here, the first is that no matter how anointed you are or how great your followers think you are, you can always do something to cause them to want to kill you. No one is immune to the fickle nature of followers.

The second is that in those dark times you must be willing to draw your strength from another source. When the praises stop, the accolades gone, and the people you love are trying to kill you where will you go to renew your strength? The sent leader must have a sense of calling and destiny that can outlive other's frustration and anger. Therefore, it is necessary to have the kind of relationship with God that can bring strength when those times come.

During this tragic time David musters the strength to withdraw himself to be with the Lord. Instead of begging for his life or trying to defend himself he withdraws to a lonely place. Then an amazing thing happens, David "encouraged himself in the Lord." When there were no friends, no family, no one to give counsel, no one to give strength or consolation, David found the strength to encourage himself (I Samuel 30:6).

As cliché as it is, David pulled himself up by his bootstraps. He went out and sought the Lord. The odds, the men, the flesh, his strength were all against him, but he knew where his true strength was, it was in the Lord. He mustered the courage to ask the Lord a question. He asked the Lord if he should pursue, then he asked if he would overcome and the Lord responded in the affirmative.

Great! David heard from God, but imagine the difficulty of the situation David now faced. He was going to have to go back to the same men that wanted to kill him and tell them he received a word from the Lord – a word that involved him taking them into another battle. Did I mention that these men were already physically and emotionally exhausted! What courage, what audacity, what hope, what faith, this was an incredible act of leadership on David's part and an incredible act of faith on the part of his men. To go back and lead a hostile group of followers – only a person who knows and is completely confident in their calling and in their God can do this. He went back to his weary, angry, and hurting men and somehow got them motivated to fight for what was stolen from them.

David and his men pursued the raiders, regained their wives, their children, and their belongings and as a bonus plundered the enemy. This was only possible because David knew how to seek the Lord in the face of danger, disloyalty, distrust, fatigue, and uncertainty. David's followers completely lost faith and completely lost hope. If there is a better example for why people need leaders

I don't know what it is. If David would have surrendered to the popularity poll of his men his life, legacy, and story would have ended right then and there.

What a powerful model for anyone today. We have all heard the statement, "when the going gets tough, the tough get going," this was beyond "tough" it was impossible. Only by reliance on God, and the knowledge that the joy of the Lord is our strength was David able to go on. David was refreshed and renewed mentally and physically because he "sought the Lord." He entered into God's presence and was able to use the strength of the Lord to go back and face his men and convince them to pursue their enemies. Leaders today need to realize the power behind encouraging yourself in the Lord; it can make a difference between success and failure.

David and Saul: Natural vs. spiritual traits

We have already identified many differences between David and Saul. One additional distinction between Saul and David was the fact that David acknowledged his weaknesses and sin while Saul made excuses for his. We should not forget that Saul was God's chosen for the people of Israel. Saul could have been a good a king if he had controlled his fear, jealousy, and pride, but his biggest failure was not acknowledging his sin.

Repentance and accepting responsibility are the distinguishing marks of an authentic leader. God can always work with a person who accepts the consequences of their actions. The second you cannot acknowledge your faults you are no longer fit for service, and tragically this issue is what contributed to Saul's fate. When David made mistakes, and he did, the Bible tells us he repented. When Saul made mistakes, he made excuses (I Samuel 15:24-25).

Imagine with me, for a moment, the irony of the scene as Goliath taunted the Israelites every day. Here is Saul, who himself the Bible says was a head taller than all the other Israelites. Saul was a literal giant among his own people. He was their champion and king. Remember that the Israelites did sing praises to him for killing his thousands. He must have felt frustration, anxiety, and cowardice as this Philistine mocked his God and his people. It is likely he often played out in his mind the scenario of killing Goliath. However, he was not able to do it because of his fear. Saul's fear of failure and of looking like a fool outweighed his conviction, faith, and resourcefulness. Saul allowed himself to think he had too much to lose.

I am convinced that Saul noted a unique quality in David. This quality was faith and conviction. These two qualities are the ingredients of bravery. Saul must have been an intimidating man, handsome, and tall, and not to mention the fact that he was a warrior king who killed thousands. But here is David, a boy, with moxie and an infectious faith and belief. This distinguished David from Saul. Saul had the natural traits to lead, but David had the spiritual traits to lead, and was able to learn the natural traits later.

Mastering transition

Let's face it change is not always fun, few people like it and even fewer people look forward to it. What makes change so hard is overcoming inertia. In fact, it is not difficult to change, it is just easier to stay the way you are. Ironically, no one really stays the way they are. When a certain point is reached it is impossible to stay there. So instead of expending the energy to make a smooth transition, most people will use what energy to resist the change. Mistakenly thinking they are fighting to stay where they want to be. The irony is that either way, promoting change or resisting change energy is spent. One of the most difficult aspects of life is the fact that we all must deal with times and seasons of transition. For leaders rest form change is rare. Someone must be a champion for change. Apostolically-minded leaders are often that champion.

God's idea of change is nothing less than innovation.

I do not mean the type of change that God resists (Malachi 3:6); nor do I mean you are to be the kind of person "given to change" that Proverbs 24:21 warn us about. When God initiates change it is not like the human effort of trying to overcome the status quo. When God is involved in change He does something brand new, never before seen, He changes the old thing into a completely new thing. God's idea of change is nothing less than innovation. That is why people love innovation – because at the heart of innovation is the nature of God and whether people know it or not they crave it. Mankind tries to change, while holding on to bits of the past as points of reference, but God is an innovator who completely leaves the past.

The Bible is clear that God does not change. The exciting news is that He innovates! Innovation is part of God's nature and character so we are naturally inclined towards it, whereas God resists change, so we too being in His image have a hard time with change. David was an innovator. This is the type of "change" God gets behind, the type of change that requires something completely new. Jettisoning the old and embracing the new is the name of the game.

One of the best pictures of David's capacity to innovate we see in 1 Chronicles 12:23-38. Here David is about to be made king over all Israel. We see a picture of a dramatic and holistic change; a transition from Saul's rule and kingdom to David's. Saul's rule was symbolic of all that was wrong with Israel; it was motivated and driven by jealousy, fear of failure, and divination. David was bringing a rule that was motivated by teamwork, the fear of the Lord, and submission to God's Word. David's rule was a complete change from Saul's in every way. This was such a dramatic transformation, nothing like David's rule had ever been seen in Israel before or since. Like all true change it required the buy-in of everybody. David had this buy-in from all the people (1 Chronicles 12:40). David's kingdom and style of rule were innovations in Israel.

Mankind tries to change, while holding on to bits of the past as points of reference, but God is an innovator who completely leaves the past.

Elements of innovation

But before this innovation was successful there were certain things that needed to be set in place. All of the tribes of Israel sent delegates to help in this innovation. In other words, it was a wholesale apostolic ambush. All the tribes sent people. The talents and skills these delegates brought to David are symbolic of what a leader needs to bring about successful transition. Each of the tribes contributes something unique that helped David successfully transition. If you read all of the verses in their context from 1 Chronicles 12, you will find that several of the tribes sent men who the Bible describes as "men of valor," "valiant warriors," or "mighty men of valor." Obviously, innovation requires valor.

Today we might say bravery, courage, or moxie. Regardless of the descriptor you choose, innovation must be accompanied by bravery and courage. This bravery needs to run deep. It is not enough for only the leader to have courage, but the leader must instill courage in the hearts of the people.

The second attribute that the people of Israel contributed to David was the ability to understand the times and then know what to do about it (vs. 32). This is perhaps the most overlooked aspect of what is needed for innovation. Understanding the times and knowing what to do imply contextual intelligence. Contextual intelligence is being aware of all the factors that are contributing to a situation then knowing how to behave appropriately – or intelligently – in light of those factors. It is not enough just to discern the times. You must also know how to respond in light of that discernment. Knowledge must be followed by appropriate action. The true test that someone has learned something is to observe new behavior. The sons of Issachar operated in this level of discernment and added value by knowing what to do with what they discerned. Being able to discern what is happening is the easier of the two. The more difficult is knowing what to do after you have discerned what is happening. David had people on his team who could do both.

The third element David needed to transition well was skill, or in today's language competency. The tribes sent men who were experts in the use of every kind of weapon of war; the shield, spear, and bow. This speaks directly to the element of ability. David's team consisted of men who were competent in what they were trained to do! No innovation effort can be successful without a team who is competent and able.

The final element that David needed to implement innovation were men who could "keep rank," "keep battle formation," and were "stouthearted" (i.e., loyal). This attribute represents submission to authority and a proper perspective of your role and position. Far too often many of us are tempted to overinflate our self-worth and importance. Far too often we fall prey to the notion that I should be the one calling the shots or I should be the one pitching the ideas, or I should be the one giving the advice. Successful innovation requires team members who are loyal and know how to keep rank.

To summarize, innovative transformation requires that every leader build a team who embrace the following behaviors:
1. Bravery and courage in the face of the unknown.
2. Discernment and critical thinking in decision making.
3. Technical skill and competence.
4. Acceptance of their role and responsibility.

Repentance and responsibility

There are many other attributes of David that speak of his leadership and sentness, some I have mentioned, others I have not. But, one more needs to be mentioned. David did make mistakes, he submitted to pride and took a census of his kingdom, he erred as a father in raising Absalom, and he even committed murder and adultery. David experienced success in spite of his failures because he repented and accepted the consequences of his actions. This is what the Lord requires from all the leaders He sends, whether to the church or into the marketplace and is definitely something that causes one to stand out in a crowd.

No one can lead anyone anywhere without God's grace. It is all by grace – even leadership. David did not allow his failures to hold him back. He demonstrated that by being quick to accept responsibility for his actions and quickly repented. Would-to-God that every leader would realize failure is inevitable. It is futile to constantly spin your wheels to avoid failure. David failed, acknowledged it, repented, learned his lessons and moved on to continue to lead. This is why God could continue to use him and why God continued to bless him. There were no cover-ups, he admitted his wrongs, accepted his punishments and moved on. What a refreshing picture of leadership and what model for all leaders everywhere. Do the right thing, when you fail do not be shocked; when you see other leaders fail, do not be shocked; simply acknowledge the failure, learn what you can learn, repent, know there will be consequences, accept God's forgiveness, submit to necessary discipline, and move on.

11

Apostolic Assignment of Samuel

Samuel also said to Saul, The Lord sent me to anoint you king over His people, over Israel. Now therefore, heed the voice of the words of the Lord. I Samuel 15:1

If you are a leader in any capacity it is hard not to be inspired by Samuel's life. His life is an example of the importance of being able to transition well and serve unselfishly. Leaders need to be able to recognize the necessity and importance of handling change gracefully. For any leader, this kind of flexibility is a must.

Samuel demonstrated this type of unselfish leadership when God asked him to appoint his own successor while he was still a capable judge. God asked Samuel to give part of his authority to a new and unproven king and then to help transition a nation to an entirely different system of government. Samuel had the task of transitioning a nation from the rule of the judges to the rule of kings; a system of government that – by the way – God wasn't very fond of and was completely foreign to Samuel. He moved a nation into uncharted territory. A hallmark of an apostolic leader.

Samuel gave his authority to Saul. Unfortunately, just one generation later Saul, when faced with his predecessor, tried to kill him. Like Saul, lesser leaders when faced with future leaders who carry an apostolic assignment often fall victim to jealousy and resentment. No one knows if Samuel may have been tempted by jealousy, but regardless we know that when the time came he did not become prey to the desire to keep his position of power. He knew his authority came from elsewhere.

Samuel's crazy life and godly mother

One of the things we know about Samuel is that he did not have a normal childhood. After he was weaned he was given by his mother to be raised in the temple, by a priest who, we know from reading the rest of the story, was not a good father. We cannot speculate as to the condition of Samuel's emotional state as a young boy, but what we do know is that Samuel's parents gave him away to be raised by someone who was not a very capable parent and that his adoptive brothers were rebellious and disrespectful scoundrels. In spite of what could be construed as a less than ideal environment for a young boy to be raised let us not forget he grew up in the presence of God. An obvious understatement, but that's a big plus! Samuel had experiences with God that the other children – who did have parents – were not privileged to experience. So somehow I think Samuel was fine – the proof of that is the fact that he earned respect and influence with God, a nation, and kings.

Samuel's life and leadership prowess are proof that we are not only a product of your past. Like Samuel, apostolically-minded leaders are able to move beyond the disappointments of the past – or as Paul phrases it "forgetting those things which are behind" – and hold on to only those things from the past which add value to the present. Every apostolically-minded leader knows that any part of your past that does not add value to what you are doing today – right now in this present moment – has to be released. Holding onto memories and traditions of the past when they do not add value to the decisions you have to make today can be extremely damaging.

Whether or not you are convinced that Samuel experienced a rough childhood or an advantaged childhood he did have a special mother. I believe that Samuel was able to maintain his identity in the midst of a confusing situation because of his godly heritage. Although it is likely that he did not have the kind of childhood with his mother that other children did it is likely that his mother had a tremendous influence in his life. I Samuel 1:5 describes for us that Hannah, Samuel's mother was given a double portion. Furthermore, the Bible makes it clear that Hannah herself was very loved; so much so that the other women around her were jealous. Hannah's double portion made its way to Samuel in spite of his natural circumstances.

When you compare Samuel to other leaders it becomes apparent that he must have had a strong sense of destiny. Ironically, everything it seems that Samuel experienced was a challenge to his identity:

- He was given away by his mother,
- Had two step brothers who were scoundrels and never disciplined,

- Raised by a man who he learned was incapable and incompetent,
- Realized at a young age that he was to be the replacement for an incompetent leader (who happened to be raising him),
- Help transition a nation out of the system of government that God established (i.e., the judges) to a new system of government that God was not in favor of (i.e. a monarchy),
- Give up his position as judge over the people to make way for a king, who by the way was his replacement,
- Watched his replacement fail miserably time after time,
- Take on a brand-new never before performed role in the nation of Israel as prophet to a king,
- Then later "unordain" that king and ordain his replacement who happens to be a boy who was probably no older than you were when you had to replace the priest.

I'm sure I missed something in that crazy list, but suffice to say Samuel had no ordinary life. His life was marked by change, adversity, and transition. In spite of all that Samuel was as an unparalleled example of godly leadership, discernment, and delegated authority. Like our other examples, he serves as a perennial example of how circumstances have nothing to do with your attitude or ability to lead.

Leaders who hold on to their authority or are unwilling to delegate it are imposters.

Delegated government

Samuel's apostolic assignment rests in the fact he was sent by God to ordain kings (I Samuel 15:1). In this respect, Samuel was the consummate leader. In essence, Samuel was charged by God to recognize and introduce other leaders. For an apostolically-minded leader facilitating leadership in others is one of the greatest pleasures and one of the purest forms of an apostolic assignment. It should not be a surprise that those who best understand the nature of delegated authority tend to be the most secure in their application of it; therefore, more often than not sent leaders are willing to recognize other leaders. The leaders who hold on to their authority and are unwilling to delegate it are imposters.

From very early on Samuel understood that his life's vocation was to be a support to leaders. This catalyst facilitated Samuel's remarkable career as a prophet and "anointer" of leaders. Samuel ordained and mentored the first two kings of Israel. He is a model of how a leader with delegated authority should facilitate transition. A sent leader should be mindful of past, present, and future generations and ensure the successful transition between them.

Leadership is an important part of government and governing. The implication of government transcends that of leadership. While much focus and attention are rightfully on leadership, make no mistake, it is a government God is seeking to establish. God does not proclaim that He is here to establish His leadership. God want to establish His government (Isaiah 9:6; Psalm 103:19). A government is a system in which one directs, as a "system" it transcends theory, style, or behaviors. A system transcends any man-made boundaries. A system is integrated into every aspect of the thing it which it touches. On the other hand, leader implies "first place" or "out in front." In its purest sense leadership is a position or rank. Positions are only relevant if the system recognizes the position as important or meaningful. In other words, a leader's behaviors, skills, theories, or styles are only effective if the governing system grants its credibility. In this sense governing is more important than leading. Therefore, it is important to realize that governing and leading, while related, are not necessarily synonymous.

It is important to realize that leadership is not the intended end of delegated authority, governing is. Samuel is a model to us of creating and transitioning government. In spite of the fact Samuel was not king, he still governed. His lack of a formal leadership "title" did not detract from his authority or governance in Israel.

It is precisely this understanding of the difference between government and leadership that is necessary for the church to understand. While the two concepts may have evolved into synonyms in our present-day culture the implication of the two words is nonetheless different. In fact, I believe that the key difference between pastoral or organizational leadership and apostolically-minded leadership is not necessarily style, theory, or experience, it is the propensity and competency to govern, or as Paul states, "rule well" (I Timothy 5:17).

Samuel's name

The name Samuel means God listens or to be heard of God. Here again, is one of our recurring themes among apostolically-minded leaders – divine revelation results in authority. Certainly Samuel operated at a supernatural level of revelation, which led to his authority. The scriptures declare not one of his words fell to the ground.[1] His revelation and authority were amazing, he served the Lord as a prophet, priest, and judge. To hold all three offices successfully takes a certain level of faith, a lot of grace, incredible patience, unselfishness, and favor. Ironically, the scriptures say that in Samuel's day the word of the Lord was rare and revelation was sparse. Part of Samuel's senteness was to bring life back to a generation deafened by the Lord's silence. As discussed in previous chapters without revelation there can be no delegated authority. In the absence of revelation, there is no true leadership for God's people. Samuel arrived on the scene with the testimony of "God listens," which is to say, God responds. When God responds His voice goes forth. Samuel was an instrument and symbol of God's returning voice.

During times of sparse revelation a counterfeit to delegated authority often emerges. This lack of genuine leadership creates a haven for managers and administrators to come to the surface. While managers and administrators are desperately needed and have a vital role, typically their primary concern is to maintain the status quo. Whereas apostolically-minded leaders are typically visionaries and lead the people forward into new areas and experiences in God. This is certainly what Samuel did. Without these new experiences that come by genuine leadership the people will die, or as King Solomon stated, "where is there is no revelation the people cast off restraint."[2] God's solution to this particular absence of revelation was to send a prophet, Samuel.

Because of the lack of revelation and Eli's poor vision Samuel's leadership was desperately needed. Samuel was an answer to prayer and exactly what a desperate people needed. He was the answer to a desperate and barren woman; and the answer to the silent prayer of a lost and wondering people who had no clear direction. He indeed was sent by God to bring hope and revelation back to a nation. Samuel stood out in a crowd because he was able to hear God and speak to a nation on His behalf.

Next generation leader

Samuel was certainly unique. The Bible says that he ministered to the Lord, "even as a child, wearing the linen ephod." This was a rare privilege that Samuel was allowed to perform. Like Joseph and Moses, Samuel too had divine favor early in his life. As a young boy, Samuel ministered to the Lord. Instead of pursuing boyish fantasy and games Samuel put on the ephod and ministered to the Lord. While other boys were playing Samuel was learning to hear and see God.

In Samuel's younger years there was certainly an absence of leadership. The scripture declares that Eli, the priest, was losing his vision. His eyesight was leaving in his old age. But I believe Eli was losing more than his natural eyesight, he was also losing his spiritual eyesight as well as his sense of destiny and awe of the Lord. His vision for the future and his revelation of God was running away. Interestingly, this is in total contrast to Moses' ministry, whose eyesight was unabated even at the time of his death. Moses kept his vision and was able to pass his vision and destiny on to Joshua. Eli, however, had lost hope. His sons were wicked and were not going to be the leaders he had hoped they would be. Eli knowing that his sons would be trouble for Israel gave up and lost his vision for Israel, for his sons, for himself, and for the future.

This can be an awesome testimony to the power of the legacy. Moses left a successful legacy, but Eli had not. When a leader has no one able to carry on their vision and continue their purpose, the leader usually becomes short-sighted and often gets lost in the mundane activities of daily living. Instead of a generational legacy God had to raise up in another generation from another family who would have divine vision and revelation. As an apostolically-minded leader, it is vital to foster leaders around you. Invest in the lives and ministry of the ones God has planted in your ministry so that God does not have to bring in someone else from somewhere else to bring back the vision. A sent leader has a vision for their current and the future generations!

Samuel was an example of this new generation of leader, young and bold. Imagine the difficulty and turmoil of Samuel after he received his first prophetic revelation, and then having to tell Eli what God said. Eli was his master, Eli was the one he identified as his authority and mentor, Eli was Samuel's father figure. In fact, it was Eli's voice that Samuel thought he was hearing. It is important to note that Eli is not without any honor. Samuel would not have known the voice of the Lord if it were not for Eli's instruction and teaching. It was Eli who instructed Samuel in recognizing God's voice. Eli had also taught Samuel to be brave enough and fear God enough to share what God told him despite how difficult it may have been.

Eli's response was remarkable, he said, "it is the Lord, let Him do what seems good to Him."[3] Samuel's revelation was a confirmation to what Eli already knew (I Samuel 3:12-13). It was immediately after this experience that Samuel began to grow in revelation and authority. After his first encounter with God's voice, he never looked back (I Samuel 3:19-21, 4:1a). Samuel was indeed a new generation of leader. He occupied a distinguished place of authority and revelation in a time when it was needed most. At times when genuine leadership is lacking God will create something new and form a new model of leadership from where there is none.

I do not believe it is God's intention to do a "leadership substitution." Rather He prefers to have leadership and authority passed in succession from father to children or mentor to student. When succession is in place the principle of the legacy is in force. That principle states, as leadership is passed down between father and son or mother and daughter there is a proportionate increase in authority. I am not implying that Samuel was not God's choice, on the contrary, he was God's choice, but it was Eli's loss of vision that caused his son's to miss their inheritance and be passed over. The authority and revelation that was intended for Eli's two sons were passed to Samuel. Here we see Samuel benefiting from the heritage of his mother by receiving the same double portion that his mother received.

The Lord's servant

I Samuel 2:11 reveals to us Samuel's true heart, "the child served the Lord before Eli the priest." We see again what we have described in the previous chapters as the absolute necessity for every apostolically-minded leader to first be a servant. In fact, no leader ever stops serving. Serving is the launching ground to ministry and ultimately authority. Authority is not given to those who assume it on their own, authority is given, and it is only given by God to those who have a proven history of serving. Authority is earned and kept by serving. There is a progression of servanthood that Samuel's life models for us. Along his entire journey Samuel never ceases being a servant, but who he serves along the way is where the increase in his influence and authority occurs.

Gifting does not equate to authority.

He was first faithful to minister to Eli the priest. I am sure he had many formal duties and responsibilities to Eli and the temple. This is the place where the heart of a person is revealed. If a wrong attitude is displayed here then you may remain confined to a "servant-boy" mindset and never attain to God's full plan for your life. Serving is a noble and worthy goal, but the Lord has a plan that you progress in your place of servanthood. Second, as a young boy, he was permitted to wear the ephod. This is an indication that he was faithful to the Lord's house. Samuel was promoted from serving Eli and the temple. We see now that his sphere of authority and influence increasing. I believe Samuel showed God his worth by serving Eli and then was promoted to maintaining the temple and performing some of the priestly duties. Thirdly, he was promoted to ministering to the Lord, although he never stopped serving Eli or the temple, the Lord added to his responsibilities. I believe he was still expected to perform each of his previous duties with the same diligence and excellence as before. Fourthly, he was faithful to minister to and serve the people of God.

Note that only after he was proven as a servant did the people recognize his favor and authority. It is likely that people knew he was gifted very early on, but gifting does not equate to authority. It was when the people saw him serving that they recognized him as a prophet and gave him the authority and influence worthy of his high level of revelation. Lastly, he was promoted to being God's voice to King Saul and the entire nation. He was the direct line from God to the king. Samuel was the chief influencer of the king. Samuel, in reality, held the highest place of authority and influence a man can hold, and as a bonus, Samuel did not have to deal with the headaches of the king. The weight of the crown was born by Saul, not Samuel. Samuel started as a servant to the priest, was elevated to temple duties, then promoted to God's minister, and then he finally occupied the place of God's voice for the nation and king. No one ever stops serving, but who you serve changes with every promotion that God brings.

Grassroots leadership

Samuel was a product of the temple, meaning one of the major influences in his development was his role in the temple. To state that in the contemporary vernacular, I believe that Samuel loved the local church and he learned how to lead from serving in the church – not in a seminary! Grassroots leadership is leadership that emerges from within and is not imported from outside. Apostolically-minded leaders are cognizant of the fact that importing leaders – or experienced specialists – who do not have a relational connection to fix a specific problem is equivalent to what Jesus referred to as a hireling, and ultimately, at the first sign of trouble leave and many times leave the sheep in worse condition or more vulnerable than how they found them.

As mentioned earlier, Samuel likely experienced an "abnormal" childhood, but this unique design helped forge the man he became. Like Samuel, today's leaders must emerge from within the ranks of the local church having been influenced by the role, ministry, and mission of the church. If the Church wants to be successful in her mandate there needs to be leaders who are shaped by serving in the church. Yes, it is imperative that the church goes outside of its four walls to be salt and light in the world. However, there is a preferred order that should not be ignored, failure to honor that order can result in ill-equipped marketplace ministers who will ultimately be an obstacle to the very thing they hope to accomplish. The "preferred" order I am referring to is this:

1. Find a mentor and serve in the church.
2. Accept training and equipping from the established leaders in the church.
3. Model faithful discipleship to others in a local church.

4. Show yourself faithful in the passion and gifting God has given you.
5. Prepare to be sent by the church into your sphere of influence.
6. Stay connected and serve in the local church.

There is a terrible misconception among many Christians today. That misconception is that "ministry" is performed only in the church or only to other believers. This is simply not true. Joseph ministered to Pharaoh, the Egyptian nation, and Potiphar. Moses ministered to Jethro a leader in the pagan nation of Midian. David ministered to a desperate and disobedient king, disheartened, indebted, and broken men, and the enemy nation of Philistia. Not to mention Daniel, Nehemiah, and Esther who also prospered as ministers to pagan leaders. Ministry is not relegated to the church. Ministry is representing God well wherever you are. It includes doing your job with excellence wherever that might be in whatever role is available; and the best place to learn that is in a local church. Seminary, Bible College, and Para-church ministry internships are good, but they are not adequate substitutes.

There is a growing idea that the world cannot identify with the Christian or church culture. As a consequence church people are being told that they need to become more relevant to society. I support being able to understand and communicate with others at their level; but this must not become an excuse to disengage from passionately pursuing a full revelation of God. Sent leaders have compassion of those outside of the faith, but never compromise their passion for God to make others feel comfortable.

The world does not need us to be relevant as much as it needs a revelation of God. There is a dangerous idea gradually slipping its way into the Christian culture, it's the idea that "church" can be convened anywhere a group of believers meets. This "philosophy" lessens the power of the church by reducing it to only "*koinonia*," which is the Greek concept of fellowship, which is one aspect (and the lesser one) of what the church is to be.

Church in its primary aspect is "*ekklesia*," which means to be called out. God's people are supposed to be distinct or peculiar; they actually are not supposed to fit into culture unnoticed. They are supposed to stand out, but not as weird or strange, but as the best-of-the-best and occupy the most influential places in society and the culture.

Furthermore, and rather elementary, there can be no "leaving" if there never is any "staying." To be sent implies needing to go somewhere, the question is go *from* where? Go from college? Go from seminary? Go from home? No, we are to go from the place God established as His seat of authority, His throne, His house, which is the church. In other words, there is no legitimate sending or authority without a local church to be sent from.

Samuel was raised and mentored in the house of God, by the priest. In spite of Eli's sin and weakness God still used and honored "the place" where Samuel served and honored the man he placed there to train Samuel. The person God has asked you to serve and support is far less important than the actual serving. When you learn leadership by serving in the church I believe God builds into you an intangible quality that influences those around and fosters favor. I believe there is a finely tuned sense of hearing and seeing that is developed by serving in the local church and being mentored by men and women of God who are called to equip others.

It is important for the church to reclaim the right and privilege of training and developing leaders for the marketplace. The church has a responsibility to train ministers for jobs, careers, and leadership in areas other than pastoral roles. Unfortunately, the Church has abdicated some of its authority by making ministry available only to those with academic training. Bill Scheidler[4] states:

> "The church must be a training center for those that are born in house. Even as each father of each family is held responsible by God for the training and establishment of his own offspring. God never gave Israel permission to send their children to Egypt or any other place for their learning or training. In fact, He absolutely forbade it."

Transitional nature of leadership

Samuel was a leader in a unique time of change and uncertainty. He closed out the era of the judges and transitioned the people to a monarchy. The capacity to successfully navigate change is a distinctive grace of apostolically-minded leaders. Samuel took a volatile situation, in a turbulent time and made the most of it. He helped the people understand what this new government would mean and how they would be affected. Once this government was in place Samuel continued to exert a huge amount of influence as a ruler. It was at this time Samuel transitioned from his role as judge to his role and prophet. In this sense, Samuel proved to be a vanguard-trailblazing leader. Up until this point in Israel's history there was no such thing as a prophet to a king. Samuel was the first.

Samuel demonstrated the ability to reinvent himself. This is something else that leaders who are sent must be able to do. Not every situation or role you find yourself in can accommodate your unique anointing, heritage, gifting, or assignment. There are times when God sends you into a place and there's not a position or opening for you. When you find yourself in a situation like that you have to trust that God sent you and He knows what He's doing, but until the right opportunity presents itself you may have to fill the time by making yourself useful in some new or unfamiliar area of service. What you can't do is leave. You have to be able to reinvent yourself to add value where there is a need.

By taking on his new role as prophet to the king, I do not believe Samuel feared losing his authority. As a sent leader Samuel's delegated authority did not diminish or lessen, it simply changed forms. Many leaders today are afraid that changes in leadership or structure will mean the end of their influence or the end of their authority. That does not have to be. If operating out of a divine commissioning and in good standing with God, no leader will lose their God-given authority. God will find a place and means by which the authority He delegated will remain respected.

12

Apostolic Assignment of Nehemiah

> Then the king said to me (the queen also sitting beside him), "How long will your journey be? And when will you return?" So it pleased the king to send me. Nehemiah 2:6

The story of Nehemiah's commissioning is extremely revealing about his heart, value, and work ethic. Before we go any further let me ask you a question. When was the last time your boss was pleased to grant you a ludicrous request? If you can't remember the last time ask yourself why?

Nehemiah made a crazy request of King Artaxerxes that would ultimately strengthen the defenses of a nation that Artaxerxes was trying to keep captive. That is nothing short of a textbook description of moxie! It doesn't take long when reading the story of Nehemiah to see that he was a man of tremendous courage, foresight, unparalleled work ethic, and unwavering resolve, which caused him to stand apart from the crowd. These attributes made the king's decision to send him easier and, as a result, was commissioned with an apostolic assignment.

Leadership timing

It's true that "timing is everything." Nehemiah asked at the right time. You might say he mastered the art of timing; but is it critical to understand that "good timing" is proportionate to the level of favor one is experiencing. Good timing has nothing to do with "luck." Nehemiah was not lucky he was favored by the king.

The foundation of Nehemiah's authority rested on his relationship with God, but it was his favor with the king, which allowed him to be sent and ultimately to demonstrate the authority that God gave him. Here we see the principle of "God anoints and man appoints" in action. In other words, a large part of Nehemiah's success depended on having the favor of an ungodly and unrighteous leader. This begs the question, how does – or can – a Christian gain the favor of an unrighteous leader without compromising their values? The profound and simple answer is to work hard; be the best performer there is at your job. Here are a few additional tips on how to gain favor with unrighteous leaders and managers without compromising your Christian values:

- Always be on time or a little early for work.
- Always have the best attitude in your workplace.
- Never complain about your work or your coworkers.
- Never have a frown on your face at work, around your coworkers, or around your boss... or anywhere for that matter.

- Take even the menial jobs and tasks you are assigned seriously.
- Pray for your unrighteous leaders and coworkers.
- Never complain about being treated unfairly at work. [Side note: as a cupbearer Nehemiah lived with the knowledge that at any time – unknown to him – his job might literally kill him... Selah]
- If necessary, take the time to develop the skills and technical competencies required for your job on your own time and with your own money.
- Every once in a while volunteer to do things at work that are beneath you and that you don't have time for.
- Don't just try to work harder than everyone else around you – always give 100% – regardless of what those around you are giving.

In this list I have identified many of Nehemiah's outstanding characteristics, but the hallmarks of his apostolic assignment were that he was a builder and protector. He built a wall for the express purpose of protecting the people and city that God loved. Metaphorically speaking he was a protector of the church. After he proved his capacity to build and protect he was promoted to governor (Nehemiah 8:9). He was a literal governing representative of the king. Therefore, in the true sense of the word he was an apostolically-delegated leader. Consider the sequence of Nehemiah's promotions.

We know that it was Nehemiah's service to Artaxerxes that put him in a position to be recognized. This is one of the fundamental themes of this book. No one who receives delegated authority does so without an established track-record of service. Nehemiah takes this one step further. Not only was he working when he was called (just like we saw with Moses, Joseph, David, and Samuel), but Nehemiah also had to prove a certain level of competency before he was given his governing authority. He had to first demonstrate that he could build something effectively. His favor with Artaxerxes help build momentum by securing letters of endorsement, but it wasn't until he succeeded in his assignment of building the wall that he received his formal position of leadership.

Many aspiring leaders think they need to have a formal position of authority *before* they can execute their vision. Not true. You only need to prove that you can serve others well and contribute something needed.

Nehemiah did what needed to be done without worrying about influence, titles, or position. As a reward for his effort, he was recognized by those in authority and delegated, even more, authority. Would-to-God that the leaders of tomorrow – the aspiring leaders of today – would adopt a worthy and noble cause and give their life to it before they get any promise of reward or recognition.

Receiving authority

Nehemiah's is a unique example of how delegated authority can work. Yes, he was sent with the full authority and resources of the king, but only after he demonstrated diligent and dedicated service. Like all the other apostolic prototypes we have examined serving and hard work came first. Nehemiah understood timing and how delegated authority operated. He knew that legitimate authority only comes from a greater source and that must be earned.

How did Nehemiah garner the respect and attention of the king? Nehemiah (similar to Esther) understood how joyfully serving will garner the favor of those in authority. When the time was right he used his influence that was earned by consistent joyful and excellent service. Basically, it came down to the fact that Nehemiah was the king's best steward. Make no mistake about it authority can only be granted to those who have proven themselves a faithful and dependable steward. Leaders who are only looking out for themselves and promote their own agenda will never gain the favor of those in places of real authority. Adam was steward in the garden, Joseph was a steward to Potiphar and the jailer, Moses was a steward of Jethro's flock, David was a steward of his father's sheep and Saul's army, and Samuel was a steward in the temple; like these Nehemiah was a steward over the king's life and he was good at it.

In fact, Nehemiah served him so well that the king's primary concern when he asked if he could go was how long he would be gone. Artaxerxes' response to Nehemiah's request is absolutely incredible! The money was not an issue, the religion was not an issue, national security was not an issue; the issue was how the royal court would be affected by the absence of Nehemiah.

An excellent spirit

When the body of Christ receives the revelation that excellence is one of our best weapons then we will begin to see what we hope and pray for concerning the kingdom and glory of God on the earth. There is no shortcut, no prayer, no statement or profession of faith that can bypass the principle of serving with excellence. Serving with excellence, being the best, having the best work ethic, loyalty, and skill will eventually produce favor. When the timing is right that favor can be leveraged to gain great authority and become a true difference maker.

Christians in the marketplace need to stop thinking about what they deserve, stop thinking about which mountain they are meant to overtake [although I love the premise of that teaching], stop thinking about when their promotion is coming, and everything else that distracts them from doing their job. To get what you deserve, to reach the top of your mountain, to secure that promotion – especially in the pagan marketplace – you simply have to be excellent. It's not God's fault and the enemy hasn't caused your delay. In the world of dollars and cents, few people care what you believe in or who you pray to as long as you are the best at what you do.

Nehemiah demonstrates for us that when believers start outperforming their unrighteous counterparts the resources needed for the advancement of the kingdom of God, regardless of cost, will be there when we ask. Hopefully, the only concern of your employer will be that you are not gone too long because they don't want their business to suffer in your absence.

Positive attitude

We can surmise from the king's recognition of Nehemiah's countenance that the king was not accustomed to seeing Nehemiah sad. In fact, Nehemiah said he had never been sad in the king's presence before (Nehemiah 2:1). Excuse my cynicism – but here is a life changing strategy – never go to work sad, downcast, or discouraged! What a testimony, here is a slave in the service of a pagan king, who could die at any moment on his job, yet always had a joyful countenance, so much so that it bothered the king when Nehemiah was not happy. Interestingly, their relationship was good enough that Artaxerxes recognized that he was not sick, but was experiencing "sorrow of heart." I am not sure, but I doubt there were many kings or are many CEO's who can discern the hearts of their servants or workers like Artaxerxes did. This speaks volumes of Artaxerxes leadership, but it also speaks to how Nehemiah behaved and the level of interaction he had with the king. Make no mistake about it Nehemiah was a trusted and valuable asset to the king.

Nehemiah (similar to Joseph) is an example of how someone with the gift of administration can have an apostolic assignment. All you need to do is read Nehemiah chapters 3 and 7 to see his administrative talent. Talk about detailed record-keeping and notes – Nehemiah takes the cake. Both Joseph and Nehemiah are important reminders of how necessary it is for leaders – regardless of their motivational gift(s) and passions – to have at least some level of management and administrative ability. The downfall of many men and women with tremendous leadership ability has been their inability to manage effectively.

Here is another distinctive that is noteworthy of Nehemiah's apostolic assignment. When his mission was completed – in record time – Jerusalem's enemies were disheartened because, "they [the enemies] perceived that the work was done by God" (Nehemiah 6:16). Here again, we see that the work of the people is a reflection of Nehemiah's spirit of excellence. Nehemiah was able to motivate his followers to demonstrate the same spirit of excellence that he demonstrated before Artaxerxes. So much so, that the naysayers were so impressed by the speed and quality of the work that they conceded it had to be supernatural. What better testimony is there than that?

I can't pretend to know all of how Nehemiah was able to accomplish such an incredible task of teamwork and unity, but he did. Obviously, he had a divinely inspired strategy and a supernatural accomplice. But one thing I do observe about how Nehemiah was able to get so many people going in the same direction at the same time was the way that he organized their tasks. No one person – or one family – was given too much to do. Each person was given a bite-sized task where the result and momentum of their effort were clearly seen. I believe, this is part of what spawned the momentum behind their supernatural productivity and teamwork.

Establishing borders

Once he received authority from the king, Nehemiah experienced extreme opposition from territorial principalities who wanted to stop the establishment of borders. Sent leaders always establish borders and boundaries for the people of God. That is why only those who have proven to be excellent stewards can be trusted with this level of delegated authority. God's borders are never intended to be restrictive. Borders that are established by proven servants of God are intended to delineate territory, bring order, establish spheres of freedom and liberty, and create places of peace in which to move and practice the gifts of God.

The enemy hates this, he hates order, he hates it when God's people know and operate within their God-given role. The whole intent of the enemy is to bring confusion and frustration over roles and responsibilities, he wants the people of God to "cast off restraint" that is why he is so opposed to vision and revelation. Sent leaders recognize the need to establish borders so that the people they were sent to govern can experience peace, be free from fear, and have the freedom to exercise their gifts.

The territorial principalities who opposed Nehemiah took the form of two men, Sanballat and Tobiah. These men were strong opponents to Nehemiah's vision. There will always be opposition

to the order and boundaries (i.e., government) that an apostolic leader brings. This particular opposition was expressed through accusations of inferiority, inability to do the task, and weakness. Or, stated in today's language:
1. Fear and self-doubt.
2. Feelings of incompetence or lack of ability.
3. False belief that you can't make a difference.

Responding to opposition

Nehemiah chapter 4 uncovers the plan of Sanballat and Tobiah. Their plan was to bring shame and feelings of inferiority. They sought to convince Nehemiah that his efforts were futile and not going to produce fruit. How ironic that these are many of same tactics the enemy uses today. Take the time to read Nehemiah 4:1-5 and note specifically what they said about their effort and their cause. The opposition to what they wanted to build was great and the attack was not physical. They were emotional and mental attacks. These attacks were intended to steal joy, steal confidence, steal hope, and rob them of their faith. The attacks were intended to get them to give up the spirit of excellence that they inherited from their leader. Thank God Nehemiah knew his authority was not his own. Nehemiah and the people responded perfectly to the accusations and insults of the enemy.

Having a mind to work... is a powerful weapon in the hands of the righteous and is the best defense against opposition.

Nehemiah's leadership and vision were too great to be defeated by these lies. Nehemiah 4:6 is a clear sign of Nehemiah's strong leadership ability. The response of the people was to work. The Bible declares that "the people had a mind to work." What better response could there be? The people caught and adopted the vision of their leader. It was Nehemiah's passion and goal to rebuild the walls and the people joined Nehemiah in spite of the attacks from the enemy. When the enemy tries to shame the quality of your work and calls into question your productivity it is at that time when you need to "have a mind to work." Not only can excellence not be ignored, but now we see that the spirit of excellence is a weapon to defeat the attack of the enemy. Having a mind to work coupled with the spirit of excellence is a powerful weapon in the hands of the righteous and is the best defense against opposition.

Positioning others to possess

Nehemiah was sent by the king with the king's endorsement, he was a builder, he established boundaries, he saw people restored to their proper place (Nehemiah 7:4-73), and he brought order and government back to the house of Israel. Nehemiah was able to see many generations restored to the nation of Israel and the city of Jerusalem.

When you consider the story of Nehemiah from beginning to end you realize that when Nehemiah first arrived at Jerusalem the city was desolate and empty. The city had lost its glory. However, because of his work ethic, administrative talent, and proper handling of delegated authority he was able to see Jerusalem re-inhabited. Apostolically-minded leaders, like Nehemiah, desire to see the people of God operating in the spheres of authority that God has ordained for them. Nehemiah was able to move God's people into a place – physically and spiritually – of being able to repossess and take back what the enemy had stolen. One of the passions of apostolically-minded leaders is that their followers live life to the fullest extent of their God-given ability and potential. This often includes regaining access to things that time has forgotten, stolen, or lost. Reminding people of their potential and their promise is one of the things that motivate a leader who is sent. One of the greatest joys of the leaders that God sends is to see people rise to the place of possessing the promises, possessions, and places that they have come to believe are out of their reach.

Three-dimensional sight

One of the other interesting elements about Nehemiah is his apparent ability to see life in three dimensions. God does not deal with time in the same fashion that we are forced to deal with it. God is not limited by time, but we are. I believe that one of the ways we can begin to appreciate the mind of Christ is to recalibrate our human understanding of time. Because of our human limitations we cannot transcend time like God – therefore we are required to relate to time, but time does not have to rule us. I believe we can best relate to time by simultaneously integrating, or converging, how we handle the past, the present, and the future. In my academic work, I call this phenomenon *3D Thinking*. I describe it as being able to recognize the simultaneous input of hindsight, foresight, and insight relative to decision-making. I think few other biblical characters model 3D Thinking as well as Nehemiah. It seems that Nehemiah was motivated by the past legacy and greatness that the city of Jerusalem once had. This awareness of the past (i.e., hindsight) drove him to have a unique vision of Jerusalem's future (i.e., foresight) despite its present condition. The city was in ruin and its people in captivity and no one could see past the obstacle of that captivity. They suffered from what I referred to in Chapter 8 (pg. 96) the "I-can't-because-problem." Nehemiah's hindsight and foresight converged, which allowed him to act intelligently in the present so that that future reality could be made manifest by his present-day actions. Nehemiah was able to properly integrate the past and the future to change the present.

It is important to note that overemphasizing the past or the future always leads to frustration and anxiety. The past and future only have value if they equip you with the necessary information to act appropriately in the present. In other words, the value of the past can only be seen with appropriate actions in the present. Likewise, the value of the future can only be realized by appropriate actions in the present. It is only in the present where the past and future can be honored, all else are just memories and fantasies. One of the distinguishing characteristics of a sent leader is that they act wisely in the present by embracing the reality of present-day weaknesses and threats. They honor the past by understanding how their experiences – both good and bad – add value to the present. Note that I did not say understanding "why" their experiences happened; asking why something happened is always a trap that keeps us captive. Finally, sent leaders can create the future they desire for others only when they realize the present is the only meaningful reality in which to live. When this realization takes hold present-day actions are no longer put off or delayed until some future date. Apostolically-minded leaders do not try to move into their future, instead, they try to bring their future into their present.

Sent leaders are able to create the kind of synergy whereby people – when working together – produce significantly greater results than they would by their individual efforts.

Teamwork

Nehemiah was a master at creating team buy-in! David obviously knew how to create team, we see him demonstrate this with his men at the Cave of Adullam. But, Nehemiah was able to mobilize an entire nation to do something that they did not have the will to do on their own. And, even more, he helped them do it in a place that was not welcoming or comfortable. It should come as no surprise that teamwork is one of the hallmarks of someone who is assigned and sent to lead others. The very foundation of the entire concept of leadership involves getting people to do things that they do not see, do not understand, or may not even have any idea is possible.

Synergy is the word used to describe the concept of the sum being greater than its individual parts. In other words, one plus one does not always have to equal two, sometimes it can equal much more. Sent leaders are able to create the kind of synergy whereby people – when working together – produce significantly greater results than they would by their individual efforts. This is possible not because they are taskmasters, but because they understand supernatural principles of multiplication. The Bible alludes to synergy in the parable of the talents and in Leviticus 26:8. The Bible tells us that five can chase 100, and 100 of you can chase 10,000. If you do the math 100 people should only be able to chase 2000, but when working together under the spirit of unity, with a common goal 100 can increase their capacity dramatically.

Nehemiah certainly did this. He was able to repair and construct the walls of Jerusalem, with a remnant, in record time. In fact, it happened so quickly that it astonished and amazed their enemies. Not only did they complete the work quickly, but they did it with a weapon in one hand and a tool and the other. This also is a testimony of teamwork. The symbolism of using what is in your right hand and what is in your left hand – albeit different instruments created for different tasks did not interfere with each other. I wonder how efficient the church would become if people with different passions and different gifts didn't interfere with each other, but related in such a way where the effort of two individuals resulted in the productivity of ten.

13

The Apostolic Assignment of Esther

It may very well be that you have achieved royal status for such a time as this! Esther 4:14

While I do not believe Esther was the only woman sent in the Old Testament, she is a great example of a woman with an apostolic assignment. No other phrase encapsulates Esther's life like *for such a time as this*. Pastors, Christian authors, and Bible commentators all have their own unique spin on how that phrase is pertinent and relevant to Christians today. People everywhere regardless of denomination know the story behind that phrase. Many Christian leaders use it as some kind of mantra to motivate and inspire their followers to be more engaged in ministry. Obviously, that is a valid application and it is very powerful, but unwittingly it typecasts Esther and robs us of the other aspects of Esther's reign that make her leadership so inspiring. Esther stood apart from the crowd for more than just her beauty. She stood out because she honored her authority and knew her own limitations.

Uniquely sent

There is no place in Scripture that I am aware of that explicitly states that Esther was sent to the kingdom of Ahasuerus, but that does not diminish the fact that she operated in a level of supernatural delegated authority. Mordecai her cousin and trusted advisor recognized that she was sent to the royal palace for the express purpose of saving her people from genocide.

Of course, Esther did have a date with destiny and she was appointed for a specific time, in a specific place, for a specific purpose. However, we must be careful not to overlook the fact that she demonstrated the behaviors necessary to prove that she belonged there. Her being there was not luck. She was not there because she won some genetic lottery of being pretty. She was there because she demonstrated among other things integrity, grace under pressure, obedience, bravery, and submission to authority.

Unparalleled valor and leadership

Similar to other Old Testament leaders we see Esther serving as a protector and intercessor. As a woman in an ancient chauvinistic society, the risk was high. Her boldness might cost her life. One of the things that distinguished Esther's leadership was the fact that she interceded for her people. It is important to note that I am not using the word intercede as a form of prayer where someone petitions God on behalf of another in the comfort of their private room. I am using the term intercede to mean someone who intentionally and publicly stands between two opposing objects. Esther literally positions herself between the imminent destruction of the Jewish people and the men intending to carry out the decree of King Ahasuerus to annihilate the Jewish people. The type of intercession that Esther demonstrated can also be described as valor. Her intervention required an unprecedented level of bravery. Make no mistake about it Esther took her intercession seriously and proved it by her willingness to die for her cause. Esther may not have been a warrior like David, but make no mistake her bravery and valor were unquestionably great.

Sent leaders can learn from Esther not to be afraid of the personal consequences of their actions when they believe that their actions are right. As difficult as it was Esther did what she thought was right. Peter Drucker, a renowned management expert said that, "managers do things right, but leaders do the right thing." This quote has become an axiom that delineates the difference between what motivates the actions of a manager to that of a leader. By all accounts approaching the King without an invitation was the wrong thing to do – therefore she certainly was not a manager. However, she approached King Ahasuerus without invitation – at the risk of death – because it was the right thing to do! Demonstrating that even by contemporary standards she was a very capable leader.

Esther may not have been a warrior like David, but make no mistake her bravery and valor were unquestionably great.

Deference to wise counselors

No account of Esther would be complete without understanding her relationship with Mordecai. Mordecai was the son of Esther's uncle – he was her cousin – and he was the one who raised her. He was to her a faithful companion and wise counselor. It was

Mordecai that encouraged and admonished Esther to be the leader that he believed she was sent to be. From the biblical account, we don't know too much about Esther's history. What we do know is that Mordecai played a pivotal role in her life both before she became queen and after.

Delegated leaders are not afraid or ashamed to admit that they need good advice. Few examples can teach us the importance of a faithful counselor better than Esther. Esther's story shows us another facet of the multidimensional aspect of teamwork. We have outlined other characteristics of teamwork in previous chapters, but Esther brings to light another facet of teamwork that the others have not, submission.

Esther brings to light how teamwork includes mutual submission. This is a very foreign concept to most people's understanding of leadership. The fact is sent leaders know how to receive advice and counsel from others without feeling as if their authority has been diminished.

Every leader knows the importance of accountability, but in the life of a leader accountability – or receiving counsel – takes a different form. Proverbs 11:14 tells us that there is success in the abundance of counselors. In light of this Scripture and the testimony of her life, I believe it is safe to say that Esther success depended greatly on the fact that she accepted and implemented counsel and input from Mordecai and Hegai (the chief eunuch).

Esther 2:20 reveals the true nature of Esther's character and heart. The Scriptures say that, "Esther continued to do whatever Mordecai said, just as she had done when he was raising her." Reading that statement almost brings a tear to my eye. There can be no more powerful a testimony in the life of the leader than what is said about Esther. I am convinced that what qualified her to be a delegated representative of Christ's authority to her own people – and by the way to the pagan nation where she was queen – was because she demonstrated obedience both before and after she became queen. Just like our other examples, Esther demonstrated her value *before* she had a formal title or position.

Obedience

In Esther we see another hallmark of a sent leader, obedience! Esther is our first example of an Old Testament leader with an apostolic assignment who ascended into a place of royalty in a foreign land under a pagan king. Even after she was given the throne she still understood the necessity of submission to authority. It is true that we have other examples like Joseph, Daniel, and Nehemiah who had apostolic assignments to foreign nations and it is true that they became very influential in a foreign government, but none of them actually occupied a throne. A Jew having a throne in a foreign nation is unique to Esther. This goes to show us that submission is a powerful tool in the hands of a godly leader.

Sent leaders promote and serve someone else's vision before they promote and pursue their own.

The best leaders must also be the best followers. Esther's life gives additional support to one of our main principles in this book and that is sent leaders promote and serve someone else's vision before they promote and pursue their own. It is obvious from that verse that Esther honored Mordecai as an authority in her life even though he wasn't her father. Even after she ascended all the way to the throne as queen of a conquering nation she refused to let that authority, title, and position go to her head! The humility and sense of purpose that took is nothing short of supernatural.

Think about this for a moment. Esther, by all accounts, could've been a very bitter and angry person. Her parents were dead, her uncle was dead, her nation was under the rule of a foreign king and pagan government, her identity and nationality was lost, she was forced to leave her home, and who knows what other difficulties she had to endure. In spite of that, she demonstrated the kind of behavior that earned her the favor of the chief overseer in the king's palace and eventually the king himself.

She had greater influence than Mordecai, a higher position and title than Mordecai, greater formal authority than Mordecai, and greater access than Mordecai; but in spite of that, she obeyed her spiritual authority and covering. I can't say it more clearly than this, the true essence of operating in the kind of authority that changes nations and moves kingdoms can only come by submitting yourself, your dreams, and your ambitions to someone who on the surface may appear to be less talented, less anointed, and less gifted than yourself. In other words, you have to submit yourself to someone who may not be able to help you climb the corporate ladder.

Remember some of the lessons from our other chapters. Moses was meant for more, but he had to first serve Jethro, David was meant for more, but he had to first serve in the Philistine army, his nation's sworn enemy, Joseph had a powerful prophetic destiny, but first had to help Pharaoh's servants, the butler, and baker, realize their dreams. The process was no different for Esther and it is no different for us. Of course, this is an understatement, but Jesus summarized it best when He said if you want to be great you must first be a servant! Paul then echoes Jesus's sentiment when he tells us in Philippians that we are to esteem others as better than ourselves. No truer or more relevant leadership principle has been revealed to mankind.

Esther's willingness to accept council did not end with Mordecai – she had multiple counselors. It is clear from Esther 2:15 that she also listened to the council of Hegai the king's chief eunuch. This fact cannot be overlooked – as it is central to the story of how she ascended to be queen. Obviously, Hegai had a pretty good idea of what would get the king's attention, after all, his life and livelihood depended on it. You mustn't forget that Esther was one face in the crowd of probably hundreds of beautiful women. It's almost as if she was just one contestant in the Miss Kingdom pageant. To become queen, and not be just another pretty face with a one-night stand, she would have to get a beauty consultant – and that's essentially what she did. She would need to listen to the counsel of Hegai.

We can guess from Esther 2:15 that the other women took each other's advice or what they liked when it came their time to approach the king. But the Bible is clear that when Esther's turn came she relied on Hegai's advice – advice that proved to be the right advice. Again we see that her ability to receive counsel and instruction from others paved the way for her success.

Sharing the limelight

One of the things that upsets followers and destroys morale more than anything else is when someone in authority takes credit for an idea or discovery that they had little or no part in. As a leadership consultant I frequently hear stories from employees about managers and leaders who take credit for someone else's ideas. The tragedy is that the leaders who take the credit for ideas that do not belong to them do so under the misguided belief that they will gain favor with the person who is in authority over them. Esther had the perfect opportunity to get a few extra brownie points from the king by taking credit for Mordecai's discovery of the plot to kill her husband. Of course, we cannot know for sure, but it is not ridiculous to assume that Mordecai may not have even cared if she took the credit. After all, he was trying to get her to have more influence with the King. But, Esther's integrity won out. Instead of taking the credit for Mordecai's discovery she made sure that Mordecai received the credit that he deserved. By her doing the right thing in the present moment – when it mattered – she set in motion a meaningful future for both her and Mordecai.

In Esther 2:22 Mordecai discovers a plot to kill the King. At this time, Mordecai did not have access to the King so he told Esther about the plot. The Bible is very clear to point out that Esther reported the plot to the King on Mordecai's behalf. So much so that even though it was Esther who gave the report it was reported in the annals of the King that it was Mordecai who reported the conspiracy. After the conspiracy was investigated and found to be true it was Mordecai who was recorded as the one who saved the life of the King. Esther could have seized that opportunity to make a name for herself and garner even more favor with the King. I wonder if she even thought for a moment how great it would be to be the woman who saved her husband's life especially when your husband is the king.

We see from Esther's example that she was not afraid to share the limelight. Neither was she afraid to let other people have the credit for their discoveries. Leaders who believe position and rank are more important than authority will always fear the gifting's and abilities of other's. As a consequence of this belief, they often take credit for things they should not. On the other hand, leaders who understand that any authority they have is not theirs anyway share the limelight and give others recognition.

Unique anointing and elegance

One of my favorite aspects of Esther's apostolic assignment is the fact that she was bathed in the anointing. While there were other leaders who were anointed, none was anointed like Esther. Esther's anointing was complete immersion, from head to toe. She bathed in the anointing (Esther 2:9,12). Her preparation was and is a testimony to all who come after her that there is no substitute for spending time, quite literally, under the anointing. I believe it was her anointing that made her request undeniable. It was her anointing that gave her an elegant and pervasive aroma that drew people's attention, even the attention of the most powerful and influential person on earth, the king. I daresay if we spend as much time preparing ourselves for leadership by sitting in the anointing oil of the Lord's presence we too will draw the favor of powerful and influential people.

Esther was, in fact, a lady in waiting, preparing and learning for nearly three years to approach the king and eventually save a nation. A woman of God sent to the king's court with a destiny to save her people. Esther serves as an example of divine favor and unique authority. She had access and favor when no one else would dare approach the king and the boldness to ask an audacious request. Esther finds herself in the king's court, but before she approaches the king to fulfill her destiny, she must ready herself and bathe for three years in special perfumes and oils (i.e., the anointing of the Holy Spirit). It is a sign for leaders today to wait, just as David, Joseph, and Moses for the proper time to be released. Without those days of extra preparation (Esther 2:9), she may have failed in her call. Spending extra time in preparation, waiting, may seem tedious, but it is never a waste of time on God's time scale it is the best preparation for leading well.

Wait for the right timing

Esther was patient and bided her time. She did not seem to be in a hurry to get to her destiny. While other leaders (i.e., Moses) may have acted prematurely, Esther waited patiently. Esther understood the importance of timing. Moses killed the Egyptian and was exiled. In his exile the Lord had to remove from him his ambition. Eventually, when the Lord called to him from the burning bush he was reluctant to go. That is because God was successful in His lesson to Moses. But, Esther did not have to unlearn ambition. She had a sense of timing that others did not, God could use her as His delegated authority because she was willing to wait.

My pastor once told me of an older prophet who used to say he had never seen anyone achieve their full destiny in God if they received fame and popularity before the age of forty. I have never forgotten that. I am sure there are exceptions, but the premise is true, wise and great leaders wait until God releases them. We must be keenly aware of the huge difference between going and being sent. One who goes without being sent is not apostolically-minded, they are ministry and destiny-minded, a tempting counterfeit. Only one who is sent has true authority. Esther serves to us as an example Godly timing. Esther's mentor, Mordecai, asks her at one point, "who knows if you have come to the kingdom for such a time as this?" This is a great question for all of us to consider. For in considering it we must address the issue of our ambition and desire to lead. Can we be like Esther, who waited patiently, submitted, and prepared faithfully before she experienced the authority of her throne?

Part 3

Do not think it strange concerning the fiery trial which is to try you, as though some strange thing happened to you.
1 Peter 4:12

14

Defending your Territory

The Philistines had gathered together into a troop where there was a piece of ground full of lentils. So the people fled... But [Shammah] stationed himself in the middle of the field, defended it, and killed the Philistines. II Samuel 23:11-12

    Defense or offense, which is better? Coaches, sport analysts, and military leaders have debated this question for centuries. It is an interesting debate. I know because I have participated in some. At the end of the debate, however, remains the fact that you need to have both a good offensive and a good defense. The same is true in leadership. Sun Tzu, famous Chinese philosopher on the art of warfare said, "if you know your enemy you can fight a hundred battles without disaster." Knowing your enemy includes understanding where and what he attacks. This knowledge is the foundation of defense! A worthy adversary will attack you at the point of your weakness. Therefore, a good defense requires knowing your vulnerabilities and weaknesses and building a proper defense around them.

The irony of a good defense - for a Christian - is that you need to make yourself vulnerable to other people. There is strength in weakness. What I mean by that is that once you know what your weaknesses are it is necessary to share them with other people who can help you. Even more difficult is when you allow someone - without retaliating - to identify a weakness that you didn't know you had. That is how vulnerability can make you stronger.

One of the absolute greatest blessings of my life is to have friends who have my back. I don't mean they are there to help me get out of a sticky situation in a bar fight. I mean the kind that keeps me from going into the bar in the first place. You must defend yourself by becoming vulnerable to other men and women who love God – even if you have been wounded in the past!

Up to now this book has been about offense; specifically highlighting the attributes and characteristics necessary so that you can move forward as a leader. It is possible to spend hundreds of hours in preparation, stand in countless prayer lines, read thousands of pages, and have hands laid on you by anointed men and women, but if you are not aware of the tactics and strategies of the enemy and prepare a defense against them all of that time may be wasted.

Know what to defend against

There are certain tactics that the enemy uses to try and distract you and discourage you from possessing the authority necessary to operate effectively within your apostolic assignment. It is not pessimistic or negative-minded to be aware of these things. In fact, it is wise to be aware and alert to the enemy's schemes and devices. The enemy has prepared "fiery darts," which he intends to use against you. The Apostle Paul admonishes us to "above all" lift up the shield of faith, which will be able to quench those fiery darts. Using faith is an intentional act of defense. Therefore, if we only focus on developing attack strategies we may leave ourselves vulnerable.

The fiery darts that the enemy uses are intended to destroy. Therefore, we must employ intelligent defensive strategies. Fortunately, the tactics the enemy uses are not creative and he typically repeats the same attack. But the enemy is crafty with how and when he deploys his attacks. I believe the attacks of the enemy are intended to bring about different levels of collateral damage. Collateral damage is the amount of ruin to the things and people around the primary target. It is necessary that every believer became aware of the levels of collateral damage. They are:

- **Level 1**: Are fiery darts that he uses against all believers regardless of their calling and history. The primary target of these fiery darts are individuals. Examples of these darts include fear, intimidation, anxiety, and insecurity while devastating to the individual these have the least amount of collateral damage.
- **Level 2**: Are fiery darts fashioned specifically to target an individual's weaknesses and idiosyncrasies. Intended to destroy the individual and those close to him or her. Examples are pride, sexual perversion, greed, and selfishness and have moderate collateral damage, which usually includes loved ones.
- **Level 3**: Are fiery darts fashioned to specifically bring opposition against one's calling or assignment. Intended to bring massive collateral damage that extends beyond the

individual and his or her loved ones. The collateral damage is intended to include the Church, the validity and reliability of God's word, and the reputation of Jesus.

It is necessary to understand that every believer must be vigilant against all levels of fiery darts. The more public and high profile the assignment of the leader the greater the potential for the collateral damage if defenses fail.

The irony of level 3 fiery darts is that they are far more subtle and less obvious than those in the other levels. Many Christians spend so much time developing defenses against level 1 and 2 fiery darts that they neglect or are unaware of opposition that may come from less obvious places. For example, one of the things that many Christians do to defend against level 1 and 2 fiery darts is to be a part of an accountability group. This is an excellent strategy and one that I highly recommend.

However, level 3 fiery darts are much more difficult to defend against. An example of a level 3 fiery dart is a high level of success in one's job where one can get lulled into a false sense of security and favor, which ultimately leads to them lowering their guard. Another example of a level 3 fiery dart is multiple "open doors," which may be a distraction or even lead you in a direction where God does not intend for you to go. The subtlety is that on the surface these seem like good things and they can be, but if defenses are down and favor is taken for granted they can lead to a cataclysmic derailment of purpose and assignment. Typically level 3 fiery darts are reserved for Christians who have momentum.

Keeping with our theme of the Old Testament patriarchs who operated in an apostolic assignment I think it is possible to identify some of the strategies the enemy uses to launch these level 3 fiery darts. This is in no way an exhaustive list, but hopefully, the process of reviewing some of the ones revealed in scripture combined with your dialogue with trusted accountability partners can uncover some of the others that the enemy may use against you.

The benefit of resistance and opposition

Through observation of our natural world scientists have come to know that for every action there is an equal and opposite reaction. This is one of the fundamental laws that govern our physical universe. I believe, every natural law has a spiritual implication.

Paul teaches there is a principle whereby natural laws are a reflection of spiritual reality (I Corinthians 15:46). In other words, there are certain things that we see and observe in the natural world that are reflections of what happens in the spiritual. I believe that resistance is one of those things. In the natural when our bodies are exposed to resistance or stress - like in exercise – it responds by getting stronger. As humans this kind of physical stress literally makes us stronger. What initially hurts and literally damages our muscles produces growth and strength. The beauty of this is that our muscle's response transcends adapting to the stress. They do not merely learn to handle it, the muscles actually become stronger. They improve with damage. Something foreign to way we think and warrants pause to consider why avoid physical stress.

Similarly, uncertainty and ambiguity make leaders stronger. David, Nehemiah, Esther and the others were all engaged in high levels of uncertainty and ambiguity that I am convinced made them better leaders! The benefit of resistance and opposition is that it makes you stronger, both in the natural and spiritual!

Two origins of resistance and opposition

There are two reasons why a person may experience high levels of resistance. One reason may be that the significance of the calling and assignment requires great strength; so God allows "extra" resistance in your life so that you can develop strength. I believe this is what happened to Joseph when he was in Potiphar's house and prison. I believe this is what happened to David when Saul was trying to kill him and he had to hide in caves and among the Philistines. I believe this is what happened to Moses when he was exiled to Midian. In other words, the greater the leadership success or the more significant the apostolic assignment the more severe or subtle the resistance from the enemy.

Do not mistake subtly for something that is easy to defeat or overcome. The enemy's subtle attacks are often the most ferocious. Therefore, your defense must be especially diligent and your guard even more alert. When defenses fail in a high-stakes situation collateral damage is usually the greatest. On the other hand, when defenses hold in high-stake situations there is a reciprocal increase in blessing, favor, and momentum for the kingdom of God. The principle is that the greater resistance and opposition that you experience the stronger you will become as a result of enduring that opposition. Some preachers say it like this – the level of opposition you are facing today is proportionate to the level of breakthrough you will experience tomorrow. Unfortunately, there is a second reason for high levels of resistance, which is less comforting.

The second reason resistance can seem so difficult is because you avoided pain or difficult decisions, which consequently left you weak and untrained. Let me explain it to you like this; when someone avoids exercise (or resistance) their entire life and then is asked to compete in an athletic event they are likely to lose, and it should be no surprise when they do. However, to someone who exercises against resistance regularly, that same competition is easier. In other words, sometimes opposition seems strong because you have avoided or even ran away from lesser challenges. You may have unwittingly allowed yourself to become lazy and weak by neglecting to make the difficult decision earlier on in your life. I believe this is what happened to Saul and even Eli's sons. For example, the opposition Saul experienced was no greater than David's, but because Saul avoided dealing with his own sin he became weak and unable to secure the victory. On the other hand, when David experienced the resistance of sin he dealt with it immediately and became stronger.

When you fail to deal with your own heart an otherwise normal level of resistance appears to be disproportionate to the actual level of opposition you are experiencing. When that happens you may be tempted to tell yourself that the resistance you are experiencing is more than what others experience. This is false. The fact is they are just stronger (not spiritually better) just stronger due to their resistance training. Therefore, they can move through it with less effort. That may not be a very comforting thought, but it is true and you should not let yourself be embittered toward others because of it or use it as an excuse to compare your circumstances to someone else's. Think of the exercise illustration. A trained person has a much easier time lifting 45 lb. dumbbells than an untrained person despite both experiencing the same resistance.

Don't be naïve. Sometimes resistance seems heavy because you have been a spiritual couch potato too long.

The challenge before you is to ask if the level of opposition I am experiencing is because of a great breakthrough that is about to happen? Or, is it – in all honesty – because I have not taken the time to develop the wisdom, understanding, and knowledge that is necessary for me to move forward more easily? Sometimes, when we have to keep relearning lessons that we think we have already learned, it is because we actually never learned the lesson in the first place. A great calling and a powerful destiny come from having proven yourself faithful in the smaller things, not the other way around.

In the end, great leadership can only be recognized when it stands against and resists opposition. In other words, no leadership is complete without an antagonist. Whichever metaphor you choose to employ – be it sports, military, politics, or superhero comic books – there is always an arch nemesis, most of the time that enemy is Satan and some of the time that enemy is us. There is an antagonist to every protagonist. I am in no way implying that good and evil are balanced or equal forces. They are not! Darkness cannot abide the light – there is no contest! However, that does not mean we should be ignorant of the plans and schemes of our enemies. We have to develop defenses that will prevent the enemy from gaining ground in our lives, and we must develop defenses that will protect us from our own laziness. Learning to embrace opposition and failure as opportunities to exercise faith, is part of the apostolically-minded leaders exercise regimen.

Understanding the enemy's schemes

James reiterates this principle from a biblical perspective. In James 1:2 – 3 we read that trials and testing produce patience and patience when it matures results in wholeness. Who knew that the trials that we experience make us stronger, more complete, and more whole? The wholeness that James is referring to means completely whole – or in other words, *without any gaps* or an *absence of weaknesses to exploit*. It is equivalent to how an architect applies the concept of integrity. For a structure or building to have integrity it means that it is solid and can withstand the harsh attacks of the wind, rain, and earthquakes – it is solid and without any gaps. A Christian who endures trials and testing and is always demonstrating patience shows that they are whole and complete, which is to say they are mature and have integrity.

Later in James 4:7 we are commanded to *resist* the devil. Resistance is a defensive strategy. When our defenses are strong our resistance drives the devil away – note: in this case it is defense that drives the devil away not offense. In this case, the best offense is a good defense. What is interesting about James's commentary is *how* to resist. Our resistance of the enemy is not demonstrated in our strength to rebut his attacks, our intellect, or in the exercise of our willpower to resist temptation. Our ability to resist the enemy is proportionate to our willingness to submit to God. The more we submit the more we are able to resist. In other words, submission is strength training exercise. On the surface, this may seem counterintuitive, but it is one of the great paradoxes of the kingdom of God.

In fact the best defense – according to James – is to submit to God and draw near to Him. James goes on and continues to give us a little more insight. He also encourages us to *cleanse our hands* and *purify our hearts*, which are defensive strategies to prevent *sin* and *double-mindedness*, respectively. Not only does James give us a defensive strategy he also lets us know the enemy's intention. Two of the things that the enemy intends to cause in us are separation from God and double-mindedness.

Defending against separation

Sin is separation from God. Cleansing your hands will defend you against being separated from God. In the natural, washing your hands defends your body against germs and has been proven scientifically to be the best strategy against sickness and the spread of disease. According to Levitical law to cleanse something had to include running water. To wash something in a stagnant pool of water is not washing it at all, in fact, that pool becomes a breeding ground for other forms of disease. Attempting to wash something in a stagnant pool only makes it filthier and more dangerous to others. Our best defense against this separation from God is the application of running water to our hands. Our hands represent strength and work. Whatever it is that your hand finds to do – your work, your family, your ministry, any effort or idea you have – must be washed and bathed in the water of the Word, which is like flowing water. This means that every day you must submit your ideas, your effort, your decisions, and the like to the river of the Holy Spirit. This is a good defense against sin.

Defending against instability

James also says that purifying our hearts can be a defense against double-mindedness. Being double-minded is the same as being unstable. To be unstable means there is an absence of foundation or to lack a true reference point by which to evaluate something. Without a true reference point, everything can become a distraction. And when we are distracted advancement is slow. Having a pure heart and clean hands keeps distractions to a minimum so that we can do what we are assigned to do.

Purifying your heart is about integrity of the heart. King Solomon (Proverbs 4:23) tells us to diligently protect our hearts because it is from our hearts that the issues (or boundaries) of life are set. By purifying our hearts, we are committing to a life of accountability. This means no secrets! A pure heart is a heart that remains open. When a child is young it is often easy for a parent to discern what is on the mind and heart of their child. The reason is because the child's heart is pure, therefore they don't try to hide anything. When a child is scared they say they're scared, when child is hungry they say they're hungry. It is hard for a child – because of their pure heart – to hide their true feelings. However, as a child grows and learns more about people and experiences the hurts of life they learn how to hide their feelings and their emotions. So instead of keeping a pure-open heart they learn to keep a private or protected heart. When your heart is full of secrets – it is not pure – it becomes unstable lacking a true foundation and leads you often to be torn between options.

In fact it causes you to consider an alternate option or opinion as valid when it is not. For example, there are many issues on which there is a clear biblical standard, but because of instability of heart, a superior standard may be considered equivalent to a lesser standard. This is double mindedness and causes all sorts of confusion and massive collateral damage.

For example, let's briefly discuss the consequences of being double-minded relative to the value of intellect. The standard is God's Word the alternate option is intellect. Intellect is not bad, in fact, it can be helpful. The problem occurs when the intellect is considered equal to or greater than God's word. Holy Spirit-inspired revelation is superior to intellect – every time! You cannot allow them to be equal. But when one's heart is not pure and secrets are kept it breeds a double-minded person who vacillates between the value of intellect and what God's word says. Once someone starts down that path they can easily fall prey to logical sounding argument that God's Word is only myth and legend or a collection of good moral stories or something to teach young children about, but otherwise has no real value for living in a complex world. Therefore, the solution to problems is to develop the intellect and forgo seeking God for insight, which ultimately replaces revelation with education. A double-minded person – in this case, one that considers intellect equal with inspired revelation – can now be easily misguided. This double-minded person, when presented with an alternate reality, say evolution, a woman's right to choose or a different definition of marriage falters in their belief and falls prey to a belief that destroys. Having a defense strategy of keeping a pure heart can prevent the kind of double-mindedness that leads to the kind of instability that ruins families, communities, cultures, and societies.

The winning defense

If you want the devil to flee you must demonstrate submission. It is ironic and counterintuitive to think that submission demonstrates dominance, but it does! The most powerful and dramatic leaders are also the most submitted. Moses was a man who was able to submit to Jethro in spite of having a greater calling and destiny. David was a man who was able to submit to Saul even though he was God's chosen one. Joseph demonstrated over and over again his willingness to submit to others. Esther obeyed Mordecai even after she was queen. In their acts of submitting to others, they clearly demonstrated submission, which allowed them to drive the enemy back!

Paul tells us that fire will reveal the materials we have used to build with and frame our lives on. If we build with wood, hay, or stubble the fire will consume it and we will experience loss. If we build with gold, silver, and precious stones the fire will also reveal the value of those materials. In other words, one of the best ways to defend against opposition is the build wisely (cf. Proverbs 24:3-4; Matthew 7:24). The bottom line is that the wise builder starts with good materials because fire is eminent. Knowing what the future will include requires a defensive approach, which means we should build so that we can withstand the coming onslaught of the enemy.

Chapter Notes

Notes from chapter 3:
1. NKJV, Romans 12:4-8
2. Strong's Concordance
3. Maxwell, John C. Developing the Leader Within You. Thomas Nelson 1993
4. Bruce, F.F. The Spreading Flame. Eerdmans 1958
5. NKJV, I Corinthians 12:18,20
6. KVJ, Matthew 19:6

Notes from chapter 4
1. Barna, George (ed.). Leaders on Leadership. Regal 1997, pg 21
2. Clements, Kirby. The Second. 1995
3. Damazio, Frank. The Vanguard Leader. Bible Temple Publishing. 1994
4. NKJV, Number 12:6-8
5. NKJV, Matthew 16:17

Notes from chapter 7
1. NKJV, John 14:10
2. NKJV, Matthew 28:18
3. NKJV, John 10:10
4. Strong's Concordance
5. NKJV, Isaiah 9:7
6. Strong's Concordance
7. Strong's Concordance
8. NKJV, II Corinthians 10:13-16
9. NKJV, I Corinthians 15:45

Notes on chapter 8:
1. NKJV, Genesis 45:5,7,8
2. NKJV, II Corinthians 10:12-16
3. Strong's Concordance
5. NKJV, Genesis 30:27
6. NKJV, Genesis 37:10-11
7. NKJV, Mark 10:43
8. NKJV, Genesis 39:6
9. NKJV, Genesis 39:10

Notes on chapter 9:
1. Strong's Concordance
2. NKJV, Numbers 11:11,14
3. NKJV, Exodus 32:10, 11a, 14
4. Baron, David. Moses on Management. Pocket Books 1999
5. NKJV, Exodus 3:3-4
6. NKJV, Deuteronomy 34:7

Notes on chapter 10:
1. NKJV, I Samuel 18:5
2. Strong's Concordance
3. Phillips, Richard. The Heart of an Executive. Doubleday 1999

Notes on Chapter 11:
1. I Samuel 3:19
2. Proverbs 29:18
3. I Samuel 3:18
4. Bill Scheidler. Apostles: The Fathering Servant. Christian City. 2001.

Recommended books on apostolic ministry

1. Barney Coombs. Apostles Today. Sovereign Word. 1996
2. David Cannistraci. The Gift of Apostle. Regal Books. 1996
3. Hector Tores. The Restoration of the Apostles and Prophets. Thomas Nelson. 2001
4. John Eckhardt. Moving in the Apostolic. Renew. 1999
5. Jonas Clark. Governing Churches and Antioch Apostles. Spirit of Life Publishing. 2000
6. Rick Joyner. The Apostolic Ministry. Morning Star Publications. 2004

About the author

Matt has been married to his best friend and love of his life, Angie, for over 22 years, and they have two sons, Nathan and Jonathan and live in Northwest, Ohio. He is a true multi-vocational professional. Never lacking for something to do, Matt is a tenured university professor, teaching pastor, author, journal editor, international scholar, entrepreneur, TED^X presenter, and director of an apostolic network of churches and ministries.

Matt is a pastor's son who grew up in the local church. He was ordained in 1996. Matt is a gifted teacher, with a passion to see people equipped to be better leaders. He is a teaching pastor/elder at Foundation Stone Christian Church in Northwood, Ohio and Director of Apostolic Team Ministries International. He is an Associate Professor at Bowling Green State University's College of Education and Human Development. He is a graduate of Anderson University (B.A.), and earned M.S. and M.Ed. degrees from the University of Toledo. He went on to earn two Ph.D.'s, one in Global Leadership and Organizational Management from Lynn University and a Ph.D. in Religious Studies. Matt is an award-winning professor, award-winning author, Fulbright Scholar to Rwanda, Visiting Research Fellow in Australia, and operates a management consulting firm where he trains leaders in Fortune 500 and multi-national companies.

Also from Matt Kutz

Contextual Intelligence: How 3D Thinking Can Help Resolve Complexity, Uncertainty, and Ambiguity. 2013 Leadership Book Award honoree for Innovation and Cutting-Edge Perspective. Revised and New Edition by Palgrave MacMillan in 2017. Get your copy today at any onl bookseller or www.matthewkutz.com

One part leadership "bible," two parts executive workbook, *Contextual Intelligence* is a necessary tool in every manager's arsenal. Kutz is a brilliant student of leadership and management and knows what works effectively in these arenas. Brilliant.

Marshall Goldsmith
Thinkers50 Award Winner for Most-Influential Leadership Thinker in the World; Multiple *New York Times* bestselling author

If you are ready to go beyond the conventional leadership mantras and gain practical and powerful insights that work in the real world of organizations, this is the book to read.

Bobby Hill, Ed.D.
Assistant Professor, Biblical Studies and Christian Ministry, Regent University

This contextual intelligence (CI) model takes leadership to a new level. CI is an all-encompassing approach to critically needed leadership practice in today's organizations. It is a must read and belongs on every leader's bookshelf!

Lillian B. Schumacher, Ed.D.
President, Tiffin University

Made in the USA
Monee, IL
22 April 2022